Glow

Georgie Crawford is a qualified health coach, and the founder of one of Ireland's leading health and wellness brands, The Good Glow.

Her award-winning podcast productions *The Good Glow* and *Soul Sisters* are aimed at helping people to discover new and innovative ways to take care of themselves and have been downloaded over 9 million times. Her podcast guests have included Wim Hof, Mel Robbins, Gerry Hussey, Angela Scanlon, Gabby Bernstein, Roxie Nafousi, Roz Purcell and Martha Beck.

Georgie lives in Dublin with her husband and daughter. *Glow* is her first book.

Glow

Five Steps
to Create the Life
You Dream About

Georgie Crawford

HACHETTE
BOOKS
IRELAND

First published in Ireland in 2023 by
HACHETTE BOOKS IRELAND

1

Cataloguing in Publication Data is available from the British Library

ISBN 9781399708593

Typeset in Garamond

Printed and bound in Great Britain by
Clays Ltd, Elcograf S.p.A.

Hachette Books Ireland policy is to use papers that are natural, renewable and recyclable
products and made from wood grown in sustainable forests. The logging and manufactur-
ing processes are expected to conform to the environmental regulations of the country of
origin.

Hachette Books Ireland
8 Castlecourt Centre
Castleknock
Dublin 15, Ireland

A division of Hachette UK Ltd
Carmelite House, 50 Victoria Embankment, London EC4Y 0DZ

www.hachettebooksireland.ie

For Jamie and Pia,

my guiding light for everything I do

Contents

❝

This is a story
of someone who got really tired
of keeping herself small.

❞

Introduction

I've picked up books in moments of joy, of despair, moments where I needed guidance, answers, even reassurance. Because a book can be your North Star, your shining light. A chance to escape and, weirdly, at the same time reconnect.

I have read to show me a way, clear my path – back to what I know is true, back to my heart, back to me. I read when I need a pep talk, a hug, a reassuring arm. A guide, a light, a way.

So wherever you are, and whatever your reason, I'm really glad you're here. Because this is a story for us all. For anyone who needs a helping hand or to find a new way. For anyone who's tired of holding themselves back, for anyone who knows they deserve more.

This story is for those who have more to do, more to give, more life to live.

✳

I often ask people if they had a crystal ball, would they peek at their future? Would they look to see if it all works out?

There have been so many days where I have found myself on the floor, begging for that crystal ball. I'd think, if I could just see into my future, if I could just know there are better days coming, then I could make it through one more day.

Now I can see that those dark, messy, unbearable rock-bottom moments can be a gift. They come to show us a better way. So why do we spend our lives trying to avoid them?

They come to remind us that life passes in the blink of an eye and to remind us how precious we really are.

My rock bottom arrived like a tornado. It shattered my life into a million pieces. My heart shattered into a million more. And as I stood, left with utter destruction, I promised myself that, no matter what it took, I would put it all back together. *Exactly* the way it was.

But soon it became clear that it was never supposed to be rebuilt the same way because I was never supposed to go back.

Being told I had breast cancer in 2017, when I was thirty-two, felt like cruel timing – my precious seven-month-old baby, my beautiful family, my wonderful life. Then the darkness came. The mornings where my tears started falling before I had a chance to even open my eyes. The stab in the heart when I remembered.

I longed for my carefree, innocent self. Even now, five years later, sometimes I'll get a split second where I wish I could go back. But it's only a moment in time, because now I can see that before I got sick I was completely and utterly frozen.

Fear and doubt ruled my life.

I was so afraid of losing *everything* that I did *nothing*.

Life stayed the same for me year after year – the only thing that changed was the internal voice. As time passed, I became harder on myself. You see, I could never be really comfortable with who I was. I couldn't be alone with my thoughts.

I was so aware of myself, but never at one with myself, because I was trying so hard to become something I was never supposed to be. I became so out of touch with myself that I didn't know who I was any more. I always had a sense that I was viewing my life from the outside in. Now I can see it's meant to be lived from the inside out.

For those first few weeks of my diagnosis, I stood back and watched my life burn to the ground. I was forced to surrender. Everything that I had once longed for no longer mattered. And through those deepest, darkest moments one thing remained … me.

I began to see that my life was built on unsteady ground. So I let it go and opened my mind to a new path, a new way. I spent many days, weeks even, physically on the floor. It felt safe there. That's where I could think and process. But when it was time, and the time did come, I stood up. And for the first time in my life, I trusted enough to move forward.

I could see now that this was my time. This was my opportunity to rebuild. To put my life back together exactly the way I wanted. For years, I knew I was meant for more, and now here I stood, without the walls, without my armour, ready to meet myself where I was. Because in those darkest on-the-floor moments, one thing became clear: I loved myself and I loved my life. This was my opportunity to learn to live from the inside out.

Over the course of this book I want to share with you how I went from revolving every day – waiting for my life to begin and waiting to have belief in myself – to truly living, discovering my true potential and transforming my life. Everything changed when I quit people-pleasing, connected with myself, embraced curiosity, created real change and began to trust life enough to stay open. But I couldn't have done any of these things without the others.

We get so used to rejecting our true selves and ignoring our inner voice that we become unrecognisable to ourselves, as we live our lives for other people. We ignore what we need because we are so consumed with what everyone else is thinking, or what everyone else thinks of us.

We fear stepping out of our comfort zone because it's safer to stay the same.

But this is not how we're meant to live.

Our dreams get pushed out, and we start to become detached from our true selves, the connection getting weaker and weaker.

I looked for external validation everywhere I went because other people's happiness became more important than my own. But when I finally stopped, after thirty-two years of running away from myself, I could finally see.

And that's when my incredible journey began.

I went around in circles for years. I ran myself into the ground. And it was only when it all fell apart that it became clear. Everything I needed, I had all along.

Everything I needed was inside me.

And it's inside you too.

Quit
People-Pleasing

STEP ❶ ● ● ● ●

"

It's time to stop
and look at the time and place
where we abandoned
our inner world.

"

I sat with my counsellor Berna, who I had been seeing for a couple of months, in 2018, one year after my breast cancer diagnosis. I had been given the go-ahead to go 'back to normal'. It was time to go back out into the world again. I couldn't believe that time had come.

There was something so comforting about that room. It reminded me of my nana's house in Terenure, my mum's mum. That house was filled with so much love and joy. It was where I spent my days making apple tarts and playing the piano. I was so happy with my nana and papa.

As I sat with Berna, I got the same feeling – nowhere else to be, just perfectly happy in that moment.

I was there to speak about my cancer and the crippling feeling I had that it would return. I was still wearing a wig; it was still very raw. But I had grown to love my time with Berna. It was approaching winter, and sometimes I'd arrive early and sit in my car for a few minutes. I felt so comforted looking up to her second-floor office, seeing the orangey hue of the soft lamp and knowing for the next hour everything was going to be all right. You see, she helped me connect with what I knew was true in my heart: that in that moment I was well, that in that moment everything was OK.

I was getting ready to go back to work, to see all of

my friends. I was supposed to be happier than ever. But everything had changed so much. I needed help to find a way to adjust to this new life. To be comfortable with who I was now.

I loved that it was dark when our sessions ended, because I could cry all the way home, often with the rain pelting off the window. Most of the time, I was crying with pure relief that I was alive.

On those evenings in the pouring rain, watching as my windscreen wipers worked overtime, I thought how symbolic they were of how my life used to be. *Just keep going.* Everything used to happen at such a fast pace. But it was all different now. I was different.

As the sessions went on, I felt more and more comfortable to really speak from my heart. To go further than the cancer. To go way back.

I told Berna that I always had this feeling of 'surviving' – you know, just getting to the next day. I never really enjoyed anything in between. Even on holidays, I could never fully relax.

Berna would bring me back to when I was a little girl. And reminded me of the years when I would give myself pep talks. You see, my parents had broken up when I was teeny tiny, less than two years old. And they shared me. I don't think it was an easy time for either of them. This was the eighties, where separation was difficult to navigate. When I think back to that time, it's almost like I was loved too much. They both wanted me all the time!

But with their separation came a lot of moving around for me, and the strangest thing was that I had two names. I was Georgie to my mum and Georgina to my dad. I wanted to be Georgie all the time, but I guess that's where the people-pleasing started. I love both of my parents very much. But I felt like two different people. I had two houses, two wardrobes, two sets of toys, two of everything, even two identities. One way in one house, another way in the other. That's just how I rolled back then.

As a little girl, I was obsessed with my mum. She felt like all I ever needed. And I suppose it would have been easier to have one home, one base. My mum was, and still is, everything to me. My best friend. But I never wanted to, could never, hurt my dad's feelings. Instead, I sacrificed my own. I couldn't find the words to say how I really felt. Because I was too afraid of letting anyone down. And so, the pep talks came, where I would tell myself to sacrifice my own feelings for the sake of others, that I would be OK no matter what, once I didn't let anyone down.

My parents had fifty-fifty custody and swapped me over every couple of days. Over and back, over and back. To different sides of the city.

I was so envious of kids in my class who didn't know what day it was, because I *always* had to know what day it was — I always had to know where I was headed next. My guard never dropped; I could never just be. It was like there was a clock over my head, counting down the minutes until I became the other version of myself. So I never let myself get too happy or too comfortable. I'd have to leave halfway through a day of fun with my cousins or straight after a family dinner to go to my dad's house. On the move again.

So as I moved through life, I transitioned from adult-pleaser to people-pleaser. I hated confrontation, the feeling of someone being disappointed in me, the feeling of letting anyone down. My entire life revolved around whatever job I had at the time. I pushed and pushed myself and sacrificed my own needs and happiness for others. I kept going until one day it went bang. That's when I had no option but to let everything fall to the ground.

It's probably pretty obvious now that I had a lot of unresolved trauma. I protected myself by building an identity that I thought people would love, intent on keeping everyone else happy – so much so that I lost all sense of who I was deep down and what it was I needed from life.

I couldn't be with myself fully, either, because I didn't want to deal with the feelings of insecurity and uncertainty. So I numbed myself by being busy all the time. It was easier to push the feelings away and distract myself than it was to really sit down and process all of the ups and downs I had dealt with along the way.

When I think of my childhood, nothing bad happened to me. I was loved and taken care of. But not using my voice from a young age definitely carried through to my later years. So much so that when I thought about not using my voice and the feelings associated with that, I would feel it physically. It was like having a lump in my throat but it was so big I couldn't breathe. As I grew up and moved into my twenties, instead of questioning this and seeing why it was happening, I would just push the feelings away.

You may be familiar with the book *The Body Keeps The Score* by Bessel van der Kolk. In it, van der Kolk examines how trauma can reshape the body and the brain and can negatively affect our minds and bodies. That's the problem with burying our trauma and our pain. When we allow those feelings to drop deeper and deeper they have no way to escape and they embed themselves deep within.

So my evenings with Berna involved going back to that little girl and releasing all of those feelings and stories. Then I could see everything with a brand new perspective. And that set me free, a little bit more at a time. I got to go back to that little girl and tell her that everything worked out better than she could have imagined, that I didn't have to worry or carry so much. And with that, I gave myself permission to move into my new chapter.

In 2003, I studied Tourism and French in DIT in Cathal Brugha Street in Dublin. I didn't have a word of French and I had absolutely no idea what I was doing there. However, instead of bidding an *au revoir* to DIT, I stuck in there for three years. My three friends in DIT were brilliant – we had such a laugh. I really needed them. In fact, I needed them a lot more than they needed me.

I remember driving in for my 9 a.m. lectures and texting them from the car. If they hadn't made it that day, I would just turn around and drive home. Madness, I know, but I simply didn't have the confidence to walk into a lecture hall on my own. I was far too self-conscious. Deep down, terrified of rejection and being on my own.

When I think back to that time, I feel like an entirely different person. After three years I dropped out, and my mum helped and encouraged me to study journalism in Dublin Business School. There I met Audrey and Rebecca, two people that would have an incredible impact on my life. Rebecca has taught me so much and Audrey is like the sister I never had. I went from failing to thriving. I loved my course. I never missed a lecture and was often top of the class – an absolute first for me.

As I grew into my twenties, I had a lovely sense that I was in control of my life. But with that came the need to make my world smaller. I didn't like to be anywhere I didn't feel 100 per cent comfortable. I lived full-time with my mum, my amazing stepdad Joe (one of the greatest people in my life) and my brothers Mick and Sam. I was so supported and so loved.

I was finally Georgie. I had one identity, and I began to build my own independent life, one that I had dreamed of and was so happy in, but with that came the need for everything to stay the same. I liked my people; I liked my bubble.

I started to define the type of person I was. I told myself all these stories, like that I loved being tucked up and cosy, that I didn't like taking chances so going on adventures or even outside in the cold wasn't for me. That I hated exercising. I did the things I liked to do and not much else. I liked to just fit in.

Now I know that, deep down, there was a pit of so many unspoken words. So much that I hadn't dealt with and never addressed because I was afraid of what thinking about it might do. What destruction it might cause if I brought it all up again. So I did nothing, turned my head the other way and just ... kept going.

When I was twenty-three, in my second year of studying journalism, I applied to work in Spin 1038. It was the coolest radio station in Dublin. Their street marketing team, also known as the Spinis, drove around in pink cars handing out merchandise and flyers – I loved the idea of it. I thought if I could just get a job on the promotional team, maybe I could work my way up to the newsroom. So I applied, but got no response. After four or five attempts and no result, I had to think of another way. I contacted a friend of a friend who I knew worked there, and they helped me get an interview. I was shaking walking into the building that day – I was there to meet the marketing manager – and little did I know he would end up becoming my future husband. It was Jamie! I still think if he hadn't answered my email, where would we be today?

I loved to work. I also had a job at an Italian restaurant where I had worked since I was sixteen. Between college, the restaurant and Spin I was always on the go, but I loved it that way. I didn't like to pause for too long. I really didn't like the idea of having nothing to do, because what if something uncomfortable came up? When I wasn't working I was socialising, and vice versa. It was one or the other.

After college I went full-time with the street team, and after two years of long days, early mornings and weekend shifts, I eventually landed a job in the newsroom as one of the newsreaders.

This was my happy ever after. A dream come true.

Spin became more than just a job – it became my life. I finally had something of my own, just for me. I felt so accepted there, a deep feeling of belonging. I was so desperate to stay there and be a part of it that I gave every bit of myself to the job. I became so focused on it that I had no time for anything else. No time to grow any other part of me.

After a couple of years, I set my sights on 98FM – one of the oldest and most iconic radio stations in Dublin. It was my dream to read the breakfast news there. It was a more grown-up station and it felt like a natural step for me. Luckily we shared an office with 98, and everyone had to walk past my desk to get to the kitchen. I had moved into an entertainment role in Spin at that point, so I was the person everyone came to for the entertainment news. It was fun, but I was conscious that I was outgrowing the role.

I decided that if everyone could see how hard I worked, I would get a promotion. So I never left my desk. I never took a break. I just worked, worked, worked, barely coming up for air. All meals were eaten at my desk. The little cup of water that I would fill up at the start of the day was still full in the exact same position at the end of the day. I was a yes person – nothing was too much trouble. I just piled and piled on the workload. Often my heart raced throughout the day as I tried to meet deadlines, running from studio to studio. I worked overtime, weekends, always taking on more and more.

I never stopped to question how I was living or why I was putting myself through this. And, the thing is, nobody even asked me to do it. I just wanted to do more and more because I was trying to prove my worthiness. But to who? Maybe it was to myself?

At the time, I don't think I was quite sure. Maybe I thought it was my only path, the only way. That there were no other options for me outside of that building because I had made my world so small. Maybe I just loved everyone I worked with and it was enough.

Now I can see the bigger picture, that I was probably trying to prove my worthiness.

Just before Jamie and I got engaged in 2014, I interviewed for that dream job at 98FM – to become the breakfast news anchor on the new breakfast show. I convinced myself that this was my time, my opportunity. I put all of my eggs in one basket, so it had to work out. I remember the call to say I didn't get it. I was away at the time and it felt like such a big blow because I didn't have a plan B. I didn't know where else to turn.

I took it hard. I beat myself up about it. Of course it was my fault – I wasn't clever enough, I didn't deserve it. Those were the damaging stories swirling around in my head. I couldn't see that losing out to someone who had more experience didn't reflect who I was as a person.

At that time I had two choices, even though I could only see one. I could look at other opportunities, take it as a redirection, become curious about the bigger picture of my life. Or I could wait it out. I could wait until the person who'd got the job left, and then I could try again – even if it took four or five years. I don't have to tell you which option I chose.

I was willing to put my life on hold for years for that job, and so I did. Now if something doesn't work out in my life it makes me curious. Hmmm, there must be *something else* for me. Now I am open and curious enough to see it. Before, I was closed down. I had tunnel vision and put all of my energy into one outcome. An outcome that was never meant for me.

Time just kept passing by. I couldn't understand why things weren't happening for me. How could everyone not see how hard I was working? Why was I reading the entertainment news when I knew I could do more?

And so for years I was just revolving, going around and around. Instead of questioning what else there might be for me, I just kept pouring more and more of myself into my job.

Now I can see that no amount of overtime was getting me that job in 98FM. Because *I* needed to lead the way to create change in my life. There will be no growth in your external world until you make your inner world a better place to be. Now I can see that, now it's clear!

Around this time I got a regular slot on *Xposé*, an Irish TV show about fashion and celebrities. I was a contributor, and I'd come into the studio to speak about celebrity news. I would drive to Ballymount and nervously stand in the corner of the dressing room fixing my hair and make-up, so intimidated by the stars of the show yet so willing to learn from them and take it all in. They were lovely to me and I felt very welcome. But afterwards, I would drive home to where Jamie and I now lived and watch the show from behind the couch. I couldn't bear to watch it back, yet I couldn't bear not to. I would cry every single time I saw myself on TV – I was so embarrassed. I would tear myself apart for hours afterwards – I couldn't believe how awful I looked, I cringed at myself, I couldn't stand it. Every second of the entire experience was absolute torture to me.

I was protecting myself by being my worst critic. Can you relate to this? Thinking that if you say something mean about yourself first, maybe it won't hurt so much if someone else does later? I think we often do this without realising. We are our own worst critics to soften the blow if we fail.

But week after week I was setting myself up for failure because of the version of myself I was bringing to the show. So, really, it made no difference how I looked or what I said, because I would have always found something wrong. My inner world was in turmoil. I had no confidence in who I was. Because I had no idea who I was.

What if instead I got up from behind the couch and sat with myself? What if I questioned the bigger picture of my life? Like, what am I actually trying to achieve here? Where am I going? What am I doing? Do I even want this? And probably the most important question of all: why do I always feel less than?

But I didn't do any of that. Instead I just drove out to Ballymount and went on TV week after week because someone told me to. I came home and watched the show, cried to my mum and Jamie and got up the next day and carried on like normal. And nobody would have had a clue.

A couple of months later, the girl who booked me for the show texted to say they were going to mix things up a little. She said they'd be in touch – a really polite way to tell me to hang up my rollers. I remember exactly where I was standing when I read the message. I have never felt so relieved. Even though I was embarrassed, as it seemed to confirm everything I thought about myself, at the same time it felt like a huge weight had been lifted from me. So that's two different emotions I was feeling.

1. The embarrassment was that feeling of failure, that I had let myself and people around me down. That I was rejected by the tribe. That I wasn't good enough for my external world.

2. The second feeling was the absolute relief that I didn't have to do it any more. I was inwardly delighted! I was free, I was happy, thank God! That was how I was truly feeling in my internal world.

So what feeling did I end up spending more time with? The embarrassment, of course. Because my external world is where I spent all my time. I couldn't let myself enjoy the feeling in my internal world because I was so caught up in the other one.

Back then, I was so disconnected from myself that I couldn't see it. I wasn't ready to ask myself why I was relieved the text came in from the producer, and what this relief was trying to tell me.

If you can relate to this, is it time to ask yourself the following questions:

What in my life is making me feel good?
What in my life is making me feel bad?
What is making me feel well and what is making me feel unwell?
When an experience is revealing itself for what it really is, am I ready to see it?

And then you can begin to ask yourself the bigger questions:

Who am I?

Without your significant other or kids? Without responsibilities? And without your stuff like your car or house?

What are my values?

It is useful to define your values so you can use them as your guide when making decisions. Your values are what matter most to you. They are different for everyone, and they can change over time. For me, I value my family, being a good listener and helping others. Can you make a list of yours?

Who do I want to be?

Again, without your stuff, who do you want to be? What energy do you want to bring to the world?

Now, when I appear on TV, I am a completely different person. I don't need to hide any more – I have full confidence in who I am and I believe in myself.

As the years passed in Spin, I felt like people I worked with were always onto bigger and better things. I was so happy for them. I'd brought them in, trained them, and now they were flying the nest. And as they soared, I looked on and told myself that that would never happen for me. That I had missed the boat, it was too late, and I was stuck. It felt like the only option for me was to stick it out where I was.

I became so fixated on one outcome that everything else fell by the wayside. There was no growth. And this is what happens when we have one focus: it is hard to consider anything else. When we hold on a particular outcome so tightly, we don't allow space for the universe to reveal what it is trying to show us. Or where else it can bring us.

That's when we fall into the trap of playing the waiting game. And with the waiting game comes language like:

> *I'll be happy when …*
> *I'll be healthier when …*
> *I'll start living when …*

I married Jamie in 2015, and when we were trying for our precious Pia, from the outside it looked like I had everything I needed: a beautiful husband, a loving family, great friends, a lot of love. But still something just wasn't right. And I could never quite put my finger on it.

It's like I could never feel entirely comfortable with who I was. I carried guilt like I was never doing enough. That I wasn't giving enough. And I just kept going, always searching and looking for more. Giving everything I had away, with no time, compassion or even consideration for me.

And as the years went on, I became more overworked, tired, drained and frustrated. I was tired of doing the same thing all the time. But I just kept going, because I told myself when I got the job in 98FM, then I'd sort out my life, then I'd have more time, then I'd be happy. I couldn't see it at the time, but nothing on the outside was ever going to fall into place until I fixed the inside. We often distract ourselves with small day-to-day problems so we don't have to deal with the bigger issues. I was simply keeping myself busy with what was directly in front of me so I didn't have to step outside of myself and take a real look at how I felt.

For many years, I looked for external validation and

I defined my self-worth based on what others thought of me or could do for me. My beliefs about myself were closing down the world around me, making it smaller and smaller. It was damaging, limiting and detrimental to my overall health. The truth was I believed that I wasn't enough.

If only I had known then what I know now: when you stop people-pleasing you will change your life. And not only did I change my life, but a life that I could have only dreamed of started to reveal itself to me.

So what changed it all? It was simple. I finally found a willingness to spend some time with myself.

*

Martha Beck – one of the world's leading life coaches – speaks about people-pleasing in her podcast *The Gathering*. She also refers to this as over-giving. Martha worked with Oprah for over twenty years, and if I ever need guidance she is the first person I turn to. She says people-pleasers often feel 'drained, angry or resentful' and end up feeling 'out of balance'. Hands up if that sounds familiar. This was such an *aha* moment for me, because that's how I felt for years. I couldn't pinpoint why I was so exhausted day after day, but it was because I was giving all of my energy away and keeping nothing for myself.

Martha says we need to be aware of how much we are giving to the world, because people can easily 'push the limit' of how much we give. And this isn't just in our careers – this can be at home, in our relationships, with our friends and even with our kids!

So we need to become aware of how our giving is making us feel. Is it too much? Do we need to rein it in? And of course, we add an extra layer when our over-giving is related to our self-worth (yes, I'm pointing at myself here). Because we want everyone to like us. We want to make everyone else's lives easier. But what are we doing to our own lives in the process? And how can we break the cycle?

Byron Katie, an American author, also speaks about this in relation to 'our business'. She says that to stay true to ourselves we need to stay connected to our 'own business', because if we are constantly getting caught up in other people's business, we are paying no attention to our own.

So how can we stop focusing on the needs of others?

Five steps to stop people-pleasing

1 **Set boundaries** – One of the most important things we can do for ourselves is to set boundaries, and we'll talk about this later on. But if you are feeling drained, this is a sign that you need to hold back some of your energy for yourself. Are you giving too much? Is it time to pull back? Know your limits.

2 **Stop over-explaining** – Do you often feel yourself over-explaining or over-apologising? When I feel myself getting caught up in the excuses, I pull myself back. You do not owe people long explanations for why. Keep it short and sweet.

3 **Find an accountability partner** – Is there someone you trust who can gently remind you when you are over-giving? It's helpful to have someone look out for you to guide you back in the right direction (to you).

4 **Don't do for others what they can do for themselves** – Do you need to loosen the reins a little? When I gave up my need to control everything

– the way certain things were done or overparenting Pia – I could see that my input was not always needed or necessary.

5 **Get connected with yourself** – This is the most important step and one that we will explore in great depth in the next chapter. By simply connecting with yourself, you can open up a new world. This is the greatest gift you will ever give to yourself.

A moment to pause

Sitting comfortably, take a deep breath, connecting with the body and the present – inviting the body to rest in the space between the thoughts.

Close down your eyes and begin to whisper this mantra:

I am worthy of love just as I am
I am worthy of love just as I am
I am worthy of love just as I am

Maybe noticing how it feels in your body when you say it. Notice the energy the mantra carries and the feelings it evokes. And know you can come back to it anytime you need a reminder that you are enough.

"

Is it time to put
yourself higher on your
own to do list?

"

Just One More Thing ... Don't Eat The Burnt Potato

I was at a speaking engagement one day when somebody raised their hand. They had a question and I was eager to hear it. 'Georgie, I've heard you speaking about eating the burnt bit of the dinner before you got sick, and how you don't do that any more. How do you keep going with that promise to yourself?'

Let me give you a bit of background on the burnt-potato story, which I often use to help others see how much we sacrifice for the greater good of those around us.

We've all been there – we've spent time cooking dinner and, damn it, a corner of the dish burns. As you serve up the dish to your family, you put the burnt bit of the dinner onto your plate. Why? Is it because we care more for everyone else than we do for ourselves?

When you look at it from a different perspective, I'm sure everyone who you have made dinner for would be happy to take a smaller portion, so you do not have to eat burnt food. But in the moment, you tell yourself you'll be grand, you'll survive. You would prefer for everyone else to have a great experience, so you sacrifice your own. For so many of us, the health and happiness of those around us is more important than our own.

So we eat the burnt potato.

Then we pass on a gym class, because we have a stack of ironing to do.

Or we skip the coffee with a friend, because we think our family needs us more.

We say yes to working overtime, even though we feel burnt out and we know we need to rest.

But every time we do this, every time we make those sacrifices, we're telling ourselves that our happiness is secondary to everyone else's. We're telling ourselves that we're less worthy than everyone else. And that is not a good mindset to be in. Of course we can show our love to other people, we can put those we love first from time to time, but it doesn't have to be at the constant expense of ourselves.

During my time with Berna, and the time spent with myself, I was able to see when and why I started to feel 'less than'.

*

So what happens when you set boundaries, when you put yourself on your own to-do list, when you say yes to yourself? You are now practising self-love. You are telling yourself that you have value, that you are important and that you are worthy of happiness.

Then your world starts to change. You become important to yourself. And when you become important to yourself, you do better for yourself. You start to put a different energy into the world, and the best thing is, it doesn't only benefit you, but everyone around you.

I truly believe that self-love spreads further than 'the self'. By showing the world that you care for yourself, you inspire those around you to love themselves too.

So when I was asked that question that day, I explained that the burnt potato is a metaphor for every time we abandon ourselves. I told them that change is hard, but yes, I stopped eating the burnt potato in 2017.

Now, I let the ironing pile up in favour of a walk in the forest with my family. I surrender to the mess. I say YES to meeting up with my friends.

'But,' I said, 'do you know my biggest motivation for not eating the burnt potato?' I looked at them. 'It's simple, really. I don't eat the burnt potato because *I don't want Pia to eat the burnt potato.*'

So next time you are tempted to sacrifice yourself, stop and think: Why am I doing this? How can I better serve myself? And how can I show the world that I am worthy?

Because you deserve *more* than a burnt potato.

Connect
to Yourself

STEP ● ❷ ● ● ●

＂

For years,
I made decisions
based on who I thought I was
and not who I wanted to be.

＂

Who are you?

Jamie and I married in 2015, when I was thirty, and he is my soulmate. I had finally met someone who was just like me. Right from the start we valued the same things. He loves his family and adores his mum; we love our nephews and nieces, going to gigs, meeting our friends, boxsets. We love laughing and having fun and now, after a lot of growth on my side, we love going on adventures together. Before Jamie, I always dated people who were quite different from me. Now I'd finally found myself with someone who understood me in every way possible.

We were so excited to start a family. I'd always imagined myself surrounded by a gang of kids. The more the merrier, I thought. My amazing brothers, Mick and Sam, have brought so much to my life and are two of my best friends and confidants. But I was ready to get some girls in the mix!

But as Jamie's career in media soared, in my early thirties I found myself stuck in a cycle of doing the same thing every week, every month, every year, and I had no idea how to navigate out of it. I felt like I was watching my life from the outside, not actually experiencing or really feeling anything. I'm sure many of you can relate to this. My life almost felt like it was set in stone, that it was too late to do anything else or find another way. I just had to somehow get on with it and find a way to be happy with what I had.

But no matter how hard I tried to settle, a voice kept coming back: *There has to be more for me.*

I'm not sure I even articulated how I felt at the time, because it felt too big and too scary to talk about. But those feelings sat inside me as a deep sense of unease. I didn't say it out loud, because if I admitted it to myself, then what? I might have to deal with it. No thanks!

So I put my energy and time into my mask. The great pretence. The external. I put all my focus on what other people could see.

I got pregnant in May 2016. The day I conceived I knew I was pregnant. I had absolutely no doubt in my mind. We had been trying for six months, but that day I knew – and sure enough I was right. Imagine, all the way back then I was so connected with myself, but I never brought that knowing into my awareness. I never gave it any time, love or attention.

Pia entered the world on 15 February 2017. Giving birth to her was the greatest experience of my life. If I could go back and relive any moment, that would be the one. I have never felt love like it.

There were lots of changes that year. Just after Pia was born, Jamie left the world of media to start a new job in a tech start-up. He had been diagnosed with MS in 2012, just as we started dating. His diagnosis rocked our world back then – it was the scariest thing I had ever faced in my life. But one thing remained, even though our world had fallen apart: my love for him. There was never a doubt in my mind that he was my soulmate and that I was meant to be with him to help him through that time. It took Jamie many years to come to terms with it – only family and very close friends of his knew. And as those years went on, the diagnosis changed him, and he focused more on the bigger picture of life. He decided he wanted to move on from the media world, to seek a new challenge and more balance. I was proud of him that he wanted more. More adventure, more purpose, more meaning. He is one of the most creative people I have ever met (and who knew that all these years later he would end up back in the world of media, but working with me on our own brand).

Jamie was starting his new job a couple of months after Pia's arrival, and we had just bought our dream home at the foot of the Dublin mountains.

When I say 'our' dream home, I mean Jamie's dream

home. It took me a bit longer to think of it that way. We bought it seven weeks after Pia was born, and I had no feelings of attachment to the house. I thought it was lovely but not exactly my cup of tea. I'd always imagined living somewhere close to a busy village – I loved the hustle and bustle. But once Jamie was happy, so was I. Little did I know that just a few months later that house would become my healing haven, and there is nowhere I'd rather be.

We gutted the house that summer, but picking out paint, furniture and all the other things that come with a new home was just exhausting for me. I didn't care about anything other than my baby. Every second of every day revolved around my perfect little girl. I adored her, my wonderful Pia.

The house is surrounded by nature and beautiful trails. The sound of the birds is glorious in the morning. We have deer, rabbits, foxes and horses on our doorstep. Over the years I have hosted webinars from my kitchen, and it's a common occurrence to look up and see a stag standing on the other side of our fence. It is a perfect slice of heaven.

But back then, I was oblivious to it all. Every single bit of it. I simply couldn't hear or see any of it.

Each morning, I would pack Pia into my car, drive to

my mum's house and walk around her village or go to a local park. I only wanted to see my mum or Jamie's mum, Hazel, at that time. I was so focused on Pia that I was completely ignoring my inner voice, which was telling me that I needed to speak to someone, to acknowledge the complexity of what I was feeling – the utter obsession with her and nothing else.

From the moment I woke up to the moment I closed my eyes, I told myself and everyone around me that I was 'wrecked'. I'd go to sleep and wake up wrecked. Go for a walk and come home wrecked. Wrecked, wrecked, wrecked. I was telling myself the same thing over and over. And what happens if you tell yourself the same thing over and over? You guessed it: it becomes the soundtrack to your life.

My great friend, the health and performance coach Gerry Hussey, said something to me recently that blew my mind. He said that we often think tiredness is caused by the presence of things, like too much work or too much going on. But it's also caused by the lack of things. So if you feel tired all the time, ask yourself: Is there enough love in my life? Is there enough laughter in my life? Is there enough connection in my life?

I often think that's why we feel so low in January. We

go from joy, laughter and connection at Christmas, to suddenly stepping into what can be a very lonely month. I can see now that I went from spending my life with lots of people around to all of a sudden facing a long maternity leave. It was very different to what I was used to. I can see now that I wasn't wrecked because I needed more energy in my life. What I needed was more friends, more joy, more spontaneity, more laughter!

But, in a million years, I wouldn't have been able to see that back then. I was very unaware of the big picture. All I could see was what was right in front of me, because I was constantly in survival mode. I thought this was how all new mums felt. My only focus was Pia and I had abandoned myself, again.

It's easy to see now that I had just transferred all the self-destructive patterns I had established in work to motherhood. The good news is that we can break these cycles – I am the proof! But first, we need to become aware so we can recognise the patterns, and second, we need the willingness to break them. When you do that, you will clear the path for growth.

It's easy to stay connected to old patterns, behaviours and stories, because the familiar keeps us safe. That is what we are used to. And our comfort zone is a really nice place to be. But if we get help to step out of the thoughts and ways that no longer serve us, we can invite new energy into our lives and start evolving. And the key to it all is self-awareness.

＊

During my maternity leave, the voice in my head was becoming louder. My inner knowing was knocking louder and louder. Maybe I had more time to hear it because I wasn't working and was spending more time alone. But even though I could hear it more clearly, I was still unwilling to connect with it or give it space to be heard. I remember feeling extremely dehydrated at the time, constantly telling myself to drink more water. But I never did. Instead, I would flick the switch on the kettle and make myself another coffee.

I was maybe having four a day. I had become so used to blocking out the internal voice that knew what was right for me.

My love for Pia was so enormous that it crippled me. I couldn't close my eyes in case something happened to her. I couldn't switch off, because I felt I was letting my guard down. Because what if something happened to her?

So I kept going and going. And we had so much fun together. We spent our days going for walks, and I would stare at her for hours. I felt so lucky to have someone in my life who was so absolutely adorable and perfect.

When Pia was seven months old we decided to get her christened. I was heading back to work the following week and we felt it would be a good thing to do beforehand. Around that time, I kept looking in the mirror and saying that I didn't look like myself any more. I couldn't exactly put my finger on it, but there was something different. All of a sudden, I felt like I was a different colour – my skin was grey. My hair was different too. It was greasy and frizzy. My nails started to break halfway down. I felt like I was completely falling apart. There was the voice again, but I was still unwilling to acknowledge it, or do anything about it.

Pia's christening day was so special. It was 1 October, our first proper celebration in the new house, and I was so excited to bring everyone together. Our families get on really well, so it was always great when we were all together. We treated everyone to lunch straight after the church, and I sneaked out of the restaurant for a cigarette. I used to have one skinny menthol cigarette a day – just one ... OK, maybe two. I've got my head in my hands as I type this, because I used to tell myself that it was my 'me time'.

I stood outside with my friend and I said, 'One day I know this is going to catch up with me. I feel so bad smoking after having a baby.'

She looked at me and said, 'Oh God, Georgie, don't say that!'

But I knew. It was like subconsciously I knew the walls had started to crumble.

Three days later, at 1.30 a.m., I found a lump in my breast and my world as I knew it ended. It was the first night in the seven months of Pia's life that I didn't do the night feed. Earlier, I'd admitted to Jamie that I was wrecked and I couldn't do it. He happily volunteered, and for the first time I surrendered. As he placed Pia back into her crib in our bedroom, I woke up, and as I leaned over to rub her face to let her know I was there, my hand brushed against a lump in my breast.

When I felt it, my blood turned cold. I completely freaked out, and I grabbed Jamie's finger and placed it against the lump. I will never forget the look on his face. He tried to pull me out of the bed, to hug me, comfort me, but I was like a stone. I went somewhere that night and stayed there for at least two weeks. I would describe it as 'glazed over'. We walked into the lounge and I sat beside him. He googled what the lump could be. He must have spent forty minutes trying to reassure me, and himself, that it couldn't be anything sinister. But I knew in that moment that I had cancer.

This lump was rock hard and small like a pea. I arrived on my mum's doorstep with Pia in my arms at 8 a.m. the next morning. My mum was so shocked when she opened the door, and I told her what happened. When I placed her finger on the lump, her expression was the exact same as Jamie's. Terror.

Jamie and I handed Pia over to my mum and went straight to our GP that morning. The following day I was in Beaumont Hospital for a triple assessment. My GP had told me I would have to wait five, maybe six, weeks for an appointment, but when I left her office I rang every breast clinic in Dublin and somehow managed to get an appointment the next day. A miracle.

Five days later, after my scans and biopsy, I received a phone call from a lovely nurse in Beaumont Hospital. She told me that the results of my biopsy were in and could I be there at 4.30 p.m. to meet the team. Right before she hung up, she said, 'Georgie, will you have someone come with you to the appointment?' And that's when my heart broke.

So here I was at 4.30 on a Tuesday afternoon, sitting

with Jamie across from Professor Arnie Hill, who was telling me I had breast cancer.

I felt like I had left my body.

It was confirmed.

I couldn't speak.

I couldn't process that this was my reality.

I felt like clinging to this man that I had never met before. I wanted to beg him to save my life.

It was October 2017, I felt like my life was on fire and there was nowhere I could go to escape it.

He told me the next steps were to find out if the cancer had spread. It was like something out of a movie.

After the appointment, Jamie and I walked up to the ticket machine to pay for parking. I couldn't get my head around doing something so normal after receiving news like that. I got into the car and sat in the passenger seat, numb. And as we drove onto the motorway I took out my phone to make the most difficult call of my life. I needed to tell my mum I had cancer.

My mum, Joe, Mick, Sam and Ciara, my sister-in-law, had gathered together with Pia, waiting for my results. All together, drinking tea, standing around the breakfast bar. Even thinking about that now breaks my heart. What incredible support I had and still have. On the call,

I asked Mum to tell everyone for me, and as I hung up I knew I had given her the hardest job. I was so grateful she did that for me, because I couldn't.

Over the next few days, I walked around in a daze. My heart was broken and, if I'm completely honest, I thought I was going to die.

Jamie and my mum carefully planned each day so that I never found myself alone. Not for one second. I was brought to my appointments, handed food, put to bed. I was a shell of myself.

All I wanted to do was spend every single second with Pia. And hide.

Following my initial diagnosis, I had a week of tests to see if my cancer had spread. I went to various appointments in Beaumont Hospital. One of the days, I went in for a full body scan. I knew they were looking for more cancer and the thought of it made me sick. A lovely nurse came into the room to make sure I was positioned properly and attempted to make small talk with me. He asked me if I had any children and I just looked at him and shook my head. 'I can't,' I said. 'I can't talk about it.' The wave of grief was too enormous to bear. My heart felt like it was breaking in my chest. I had never felt anything like it before. He smiled at me, made me comfortable.

I lay down and prayed for my life.

The terror I felt that week is indescribable – knowing that the lump was still in my chest and not knowing where else the cancer could be. I never touched the lump again after that first night. I only ever touched it once. I often say that my blood turned cold that night and stayed cold for two weeks. I couldn't let my hands touch any part of my body. I was so afraid of what I might feel. To be honest, five years later, I still have days like that.

I was due to find out if my cancer had spread on 16 October, which turned out to be the day of Storm Ophelia. The storm that came rumbling into town and shut everything down. That day all hospital outpatient appointments were cancelled. I rang the hospital all morning, over and over again, to try to get some answers, but the phone just rang out. It was another rock-bottom moment – back on the floor, unable to take any more. It was a quiet morning. My mum was with me, but there just wasn't much left to say. We were all exhausted.

At 12 p.m., my phone rang on private number, and I knew this was the call I was waiting for. I walked into my bedroom and answered.

It was Professor Hill. He had my results. I'll never forget the words that followed – they replayed in my head over and over for hours. I kept repeating them to myself to make sure I'd heard correctly: 'Your cancer is contained to your breast.'

I stared in the mirror, wondering if this was real, was I dreaming? *Please make this be real. My cancer hasn't spread?*

Professor Hill said he wanted to operate that week to remove the cancer.

Everything changed in that moment. I felt like someone had just handed me my life back. I thanked him over and over again and looked over to see my mum standing at my bedroom door with Pia in her arms. I ran to her and the three of us hugged. I can't describe how I felt at that moment, but I'll never forget it. It was like someone had been holding a gun to my head and finally took it down. Finally, I could breathe.

We went into the kitchen, I called Jamie, and he came straight home. He arrived at the door with a box of two hundred tea bags because, you know, there was a storm for a day, and I laughed for the first time in ages. My stepdad Joe arrived next, and I made scrambled eggs, toast and tea, and we celebrated. I felt like I could taste, see, breathe and speak again. We all knew I had been handed a lifeline that day, and we were going to cling to it.

And that was the day everything changed.

Later that night, for the first time, I opened my mind to a different path. A path I never knew existed, and one that changed my life forever.

*

After putting Pia to bed, I told Jamie that I needed to switch off for an hour. After more than a week of crying and worrying, I needed to take some time off to distract myself. I flicked through Netflix in search of an escape, and Jamie mentioned that somebody had recommended watching a documentary called *I Am Not Your Guru*. It was by this guy called Tony Robbins. I had never heard of him before. Jamie explained that Tony was this self-help expert from America, and at that point I would have taken a pep talk from the postman, so I decided to open my mind and watch it.

The documentary followed Tony and his team to his seminar called Date with Destiny, which was attended by over two thousand people in Florida. As various audience members stood up and told their stories, I cried and cried. I couldn't believe that all of these incredibly brave people, who had been in rock-bottom moments, were discovering a way out, a better way. They had opened their minds to healing and were going on the journey in front of my eyes.

During that two-hour documentary, I heard something that completely changed my life.

Addressing the audience, Tony said: 'I'll tell you what your biggest problem is. You think you shouldn't have them. Problems make us grow, problems are what sculpt our soul, problems are what make us become more. If we can realise that life is always happening *for* us, not *to* us, all the pain and suffering disappears. Your problem is your gift.'

As I listened to those words I felt like I was having an out-of-body experience. I had never heard anything like it. I had never looked at life that way. I went back and watched that part again, letting the words sink in. In all my life, I had never even considered that something 'bad' happening could turn out to be a gift. It was an entirely new concept to me, and something changed in me as I listened to his words.

It was a profound shift.

There had to be a reason why I was hearing these words on the very day I found out that my cancer hadn't spread. This was a message I was supposed to hear.

That night was the first time that I acknowledged the voice in my head and all that it had been trying to tell me for so many years.

I finally let it in – I could finally hear.

And the message was so loud.

I am surrounded by love.

I am enough exactly how I am.

I have so much love to give.

I have so much life to live.

And at that moment, it didn't matter if I was validated by the outside world – I had just become more present with myself than I had ever been.

At that moment, I truly loved myself.

At that moment, it was like somebody took me by the shoulders and physically turned me in the opposite direction to the one I had been standing in.

Everything was different.

And I could see a clear path forward.

It was a new world.

It had all become clear. Three things happened over those two weeks to let me know that my inner voice was to be trusted.

When I found a lump in my breast, I knew it was cancer.

After the initial shock of my diagnosis, I had a feeling the cancer hadn't spread, and I was right.

Then, something told me to press play on that documentary, so I did.

I could finally see that my inner voice was guiding me. And the surprising thing was that it was right. I could see, after years of pushing it away, that my inner voice had good intentions. It was like I had spent my entire life looking out into the world, projecting. And now, for the first time ever, I was actually facing myself. I was ready to stop and listen.

Yes, I was still scared that night; yes, I was still sad. I was fully aware that my life as I knew it was over. I had a long way to go with treatment. But I didn't feel alone. I had something in common with all of the people I had just watched: the pain, the suffering and the heartbreak. I wasn't the only one. And I knew deep within that I had the strength to face what lay ahead for me.

That night, a tiny crack of light had appeared at the end of a very dark tunnel.

And my perspective shifted.

For the first time, I was on my own team.

So I started to think, *What if I get to live? What if I survive it?*

What if this diagnosis, in some crazy messed-up way, was leading me somewhere better?

What if this was happening *for* me?

And although I couldn't step into that light just yet, I could see it and I knew it was there.

By God, I knew it was there.

And that was my rebirth: the night I realised that I really loved myself. I wanted more than anything to watch Pia grow up, I wanted to walk into school on her first day, I wanted to be everything to her that my mum had been to me. I wanted to be her best friend and the one she could turn to no matter what. I wanted to watch her soar. But I knew before all that, I had to take care of myself. I needed to become my own best friend first.

I needed to put all the love I was giving out into the world back into myself. Because I could see that this experience was here to help me evolve into the person I was meant to be.

And I was ready to do the work. In the months that followed, the real work took place. Constantly checking in with myself, creating space so I could listen to my heart, and it has become a continuous journey of discovery.

30-Second Check In

We spend so much time on autopilot that we are often unaware of how we actually feel or what we actually need.

All you need is 30 seconds to transform your day.

Take yourself out of autopilot by asking yourself one simple question.

I like to do this in front of a mirror with my hand on my heart.

The question is: 'how do I feel and what do I need today?'

This moment allows you to become present and bring your life into your conscious mind.

This simple check-in can completely transform your day.

Remember, bring your mind, body and soul into your awareness. And give yourself what you need.

Now when I go out into the world to tell my story, people often say, 'Ah, sure, it's easy to change when you have cancer.' But the truth is, my life didn't change because I was diagnosed with cancer – my life changed because I did the work to change my life.

I didn't have to change. We've heard it so many times – 'I can't wait to go back to normal.' But as time went on,

I could see that I didn't want to go back. My old life kept me small. My old life wasn't working *for* me.

And I can hear some of you screaming, 'Where do I get the motivation for change?' It is the hardest part, isn't it, finding the motivation to really make the changes you want to make?

Well, the first step is to know that you are worthy. Once you know and believe you are worthy, you will grow. You are worthy of becoming the best version of you. And you become what you believe.

This is your life, this is your opportunity. Grab it with both hands, just like I did.

Five steps to connect with and listen to yourself

The French philosopher Blaise Pascal said, 'All of humanity's problems stem from man's inability to sit quietly in a room alone.'

We often run from ourselves – some of us spend our whole lives running. But is it time to acknowledge your inner voice and all it can bring to your life? This can be very hard to do. But make a commitment to carve out this time for yourself. In order to break the cycle of people-pleasing and start moving forward, it's time to get reconnected with the most important person in your life: *you*.

1 Spend meaningful time with yourself

I used to take the Luas to and from work every day. One day, my stepdad Joe was collecting me from my stop, and as I climbed into his car, I told him that the battery on my phone had died. He was slagging me, saying, 'Oh no, whatever did you do to pass the time?' And I responded, 'I had to look out the ... window.' As I said it, I became aware of how horrified I was that I'd had to *look out the window*. We burst out laughing, because we could see how ridiculous I sounded.

But I remember that day and that journey, because it was probably one of the only times back then that I wasn't distracting myself from the bigger picture. Distracting myself by scrolling, listening, talking, smoking, drinking. It was just me and my thoughts.

There is a great story about a professor who brought a jar to his class and placed some rocks inside. He held it up to the class and asked them if the jar was full. They said yes. Then he poured some pebbles into the jar and they fell in between the rocks. He held the jar up high – 'What about now?' he asked. 'Do you think the jar is full?' The class nodded. Then he poured sand into the jar and filled it to the brim. He asked, 'Is it full now?' They replied, 'Yes, it is!' He went on to tell them that the jar is a representation of life. The rocks are the big things in life like our relationship with ourselves, our health, our family – the most important things that have real value. He said the pebbles represent our friendships, jobs, homes – things that often come and go. And the sand represents the things that don't mean much to your life as a whole, like browsing on social media or material objects. The point of the story is that if you fill the jar with sand or pebbles first, you will have no space for the rocks. It's a reminder of what it is we are prioritising and whether we have things in the correct order. I spent so much time distracting myself with the sand and the pebbles that I abandoned the relationship I had with myself. I had my priorities in the wrong order.

Is it time to stop distracting yourself from the day-to-day small things and start focusing on the bigger things, like the relationship you have with yourself? The greatest way to reconnect with yourself is to sit in silence with no distractions. Because, as time goes on and you do it more regularly, you will have more breakthroughs in that ten minutes of silence than you will anywhere else. If you find spending time in silence difficult, you could start by setting a timer on your phone for one minute. Just sit on your couch with no distractions and just *be* for sixty seconds. Then as the days go on you can build yourself up from one minute to three minutes to five minutes and so on. If you can do this outside, even better. I always find clearing my head easier when I'm close to nature.

If you do have trouble spending time with yourself in silence, having a therapist to confide in about this will really help. Berna supported me as I slowed things down and reconnected with myself. She was there for me in the silence and I felt very safe in it with her.

2 Embrace silence

The messages we hear when we embrace silence are there to guide us, help us make decisions and keep us on the right path. Those messages or whispers start as gentle nudges, little thoughts that cross your mind, like, *Why am I doing this?* Maybe your job is not fulfilling you as it should; maybe this person does not have your best interests at heart. Most of the time, when we have these thoughts we ignore them because we are busy. But I am here to tell you to let the voice in.

Next time you embrace silence, ask yourself:

1. *What have I not been paying attention to?*
2. *What is whispering to me right now?*

Your life is speaking to you all the time. The question is, are you willing to listen?

Start today.

Embrace your inner world.

Embrace the silence.

Silence is your gateway to more.

3 Learn to love yourself

If you look in the mirror and all you can see are things you want to change, or you think you are not good enough, it's time to reprogramme how you view yourself.

You are enough.

Can you repeat that?

I am enough.

We often think, *I'll be enough when* ... But you are enough now.

Instead of looking in the mirror and seeing everything you are not, look for everything you are. It's time to retrain the way we treat and speak to ourselves. I can't tell you how much therapy helped me to reframe how I view myself.

It's about taking small steps forward every day. It's about saying nicer things to yourself more often, retraining your brain to look for the good. It can help to write things down, so you can see them clearly on paper.

Let's try it now.

In your journal, can you list five things you like about yourself?

Then next week, list five more things. It can be helpful to have a weekly ritual where every Sunday, say, you write down five new things you like about yourself. It may seem hard at first, but as the weeks go by it will become easier.

Then you can ask yourself bigger questions, such as: What could you be if you let go of your past? What could you be if you forgave yourself? What if today is the first day of your next chapter? Everything you do today and every choice you make is for your future self. Our brains believe what we tell them, so let's remind ourselves of all we are and all we can be. Can you remind yourself of all the love you have, the kindness in your heart, your joy and compassion? With enough work and support, we can change our stories from bad to good.

4 Start every day with a check-in

Do you start your day giving to everyone else before you've even taken a second to stop and ask yourself how *you* feel? Even if you only have thirty seconds to spare, it's really nice to start the day with a check-in with yourself.

Sometimes, I put my hand on my heart and feel gratitude for another morning, more light, more hope.

And then it can be useful to bring your needs into your awareness. Just a few minutes to connect and let that inner voice, your inner knowing, through.

What do I need today? Is it more water, a healthier dinner, some fresh air?

We spend so much time running and giving in the morning, we forget that we have needs too. A lot can come up in a thirty-second check-in. And once you receive your messages for the day ahead, you can keep them in mind as you move through the day.

Have you ever bought a basil plant for your kitchen? It always takes me by surprise how much water those plants need. I have to water mine every single day to keep it alive! So when I think about how for so many years I never checked in with myself, not caring about myself, I can't believe I was able to keep going for so long. A thirty-second check-in doesn't take much, but can give you the power to transform the rest of your day. Remember, you matter, so make the time.

5 Become consciously awake

We spend so much of our lives on autopilot, making decisions throughout the day that we give little thought to – like how we start our day, the route we take to work, the food we eat, the things we watch on TV or how we spend our weekends. The more we live on autopilot, the more certain stories will simmer just below the surface. They are always there, playing on a loop, going around and around. We barely notice them, but they are constant. Often these stories have themes of fear, anger and resentment.

They could sound like:
- *I can't believe they did that.*
- *Why is this person always so irritating?*
- *I am so stressed all the time.*
- *I don't have enough time.*
- *Why can nobody see how hard I work?*
- *Nobody appreciates me.*
- *I always get in the wrong queue.*
- *Why do things always happen to me?*

Or even worse:
- *I am such a failure.*
- *Look at all they have achieved – I'll never be like them.*
- *That will never happen for me.*
- *Why do I always look so bad?*
- *Things will never change.*

Many of the stories we tell ourselves are on an unconscious loop. We aren't even really aware that they are there. But the danger is that they can become our truth. Or what we *think* is our truth.

But you have the power to break this cycle by becoming more aware and consciously awake. When I bring those underlying thoughts and stories into the forefront of my mind and sit with them, I can see that they have no truth. Yes, I can see and hear them as they rise up, but the difference now is that I acknowledge them, thank them for showing up and let them pass through. Because I can see them for what they are: thoughts, not truth.

You can bring your life into the present by practising things like gratitude, mindfulness and breathing. If you haven't done it before, why not try it for a couple of minutes? If you are being too hard on yourself, can you list three things you are grateful for today? If you feel stressed, can you stop for thirty seconds to centre yourself by taking deep breaths?

When you bring your life into the present, you can start to make decisions that will better serve you. For years, I filled my trolley with fruit and vegetables, but at the end of the week they ended up in the bin. I believed I was making healthy decisions because of how much healthy food I was buying, but I wasn't aware enough to see that I wasn't actually eating any of it. Now, before I go in to a speaking engagement, I take a minute to sit with myself and, instead of frantically looking over my notes, I'll ask myself what is my intention here?

What energy am I hoping to give to the room? I know I will do a better job for everyone who is listening to me if I first become centred in myself.

One of my favourite expressions is 'slow down to speed up'. Because when we slow down we can see our life the way it is, instead of focusing on how we want it to be. And when we see our life for what it is, we can then make better decisions, and I promise those decisions will make your life better.

Come back to yourself

We often experience moments of stress throughout the days and weeks of our lives. Sometimes, we forget that these moments are part of being human and that we are all likely to face them, no matter who we are. So whether it's a missed bus, a fall-out with a friend, feeling overwhelmed at work, it's so important that we support ourselves, allow ourselves to feel it, and allow it to pass.

Grounding

I love to ground myself because it is such a simple

yet powerful way to get out of our thinking minds and experience the present moment.

So whether sitting or standing, feel into your feet, move your weight from side to side, or back and forth. Can you bring some curiosity into it – what are you noticing? How does it feel to imagine your feet like roots of a tree, strong and solid?

Breath

When it comes to our breath, one of these techniques may work for you.

1. Often when we are stressed or in 'fight or flight' mode, our breath can become shallow and uneven. See how it is to bring your awareness to the breath, maybe deepening it, or maybe even just becoming curious about how it feels in the body first. Then it might feel OK to take three deep breaths, either lengthening the exhale like you are blowing out a candle, or releasing it with a big sigh.

2. Another alternative breath technique which is very powerful for activating our parasympathetic nervous system is our 2:1 breath. So we inhale and pause, inhale again (two in a row), and then very slowly release the breath through pursed lips. Try this three or four times and see how you feel after.

Senses

Connecting with our senses is a great way to become present when we get caught up in stories or mind chatter. Take a pause, and note five things you see, four things you hear, three things you feel or touch, two things you taste, and one thing you smell – also noting if you don't notice anything around some of the senses – no sensation is also sensation!

Perspective

Getting outside or into a wider space can remind us of the bigger world at play when our mind narrows in on something very specific that causes us stress. Can you step out in nature for a few minutes, or even look out the window into the vast and spacious sky? Listen to a birdsong playlist on Spotify or watch a nature documentary. Combine this with breathing and it can be highly impactful at providing us with some much-needed perspective.

A moment to pause

Below are some open-hearted affirmations, reminding us of our intuitive abilities and inner wisdom:

I trust myself
I trust my intuition
I trust who I am

It's okay if these feel sticky or strange to say. Sometimes we need to build the brightness of our intuitions slowly, day by day. Sometimes we need to remind ourselves to let the whispers in and to trust what our inner voice is trying tell us.

I trust myself
I trust my intuition
I trust who I am

"

You don't need
to have the answers for
everyone around you.

"

Just One More Thing ...
Say 'I Don't Know'

One day as I busied myself in the kitchen, Jamie asked me an off-the-cuff question about something in the news. I can't quite remember what the question was, but I remember how I felt when I didn't know the answer.

I was immediately stressed. I racked my brain. I've always prided myself on knowing about things, especially relating to the news. As I searched for the answer, I felt my heart rate increase, and I lost concentration on what I was doing. I gave up on everything in that moment as I tried to get the answer for him. But I didn't know it, and I didn't know what to say.

But then something came over me. I let go. I surrendered. I looked up at him and I heard the following words come out of my mouth: 'I don't know.' That was a sentence I was not used to saying.

It took me by surprise; it took Jamie by surprise. Before, if I didn't know the answer to things, I would have speculated or started a deeper conversation around it.

But that was the first time that I simply said, 'I don't know.'

It felt strange at first. Like I was giving up or that I didn't care. But then I felt a release and thought, *That feels better.*

Then I felt a sense of freedom. *Wow, I feel so free after that.*

Then I started to think … *Hmmm, I could get used to this. Let me try it again.*

'I don't know.'

'I DON'T KNOW.'

And guess what? I didn't care to know.

'I. DON'T. KNOW.'

Are you the person everyone rings in a crisis? Are you asked what's for dinner or what restaurant you're all going to every time? Can you see people getting frustrated with you when you don't have the answers?

Poor Jamie was only asking me a question, making conversation, but he didn't know how much of a big deal it was for me not to know.

Because for so long, my thing was knowing things.

In that moment, I realised that I had set myself free. I could see that I don't have to have all the answers – I don't want to have all the answers!

When my inner world became bigger, my outer world became smaller. I was no longer consumed by what other people did, or thought, or said. Of course I care about the bigger issues in the world, but the nitty-gritty stuff that I let into my space for years, I simply didn't want to know any more.

So 'I don't know' became my new best friend. I started to get really familiar with saying those three little words. I would try it out on different people. And each time I said it, I set myself free a little bit more. I was letting go a little bit more, and it felt so good.

I could finally accept that I wasn't stupid for not knowing.

So this is my message for you: you don't have to have all the answers. You don't have to abandon yourself to look for answers for everyone around you.

Set yourself free. Try it this week – gift yourself the really delicious feeling of saying …

'I
DON'T
KNOW.'

❝

Change your energy,
change your life.

❞

Morning Ritual

These days, my morning routine looks a little different than it used to. For so many years, I started my days at a hundred miles an hour, and it went on for years. I would snooze my alarm to the last possible minute, hanging on to every precious second in bed before I had to face the day. Then I would dive out of bed and into the shower. Before I knew it, I was out the door in a whirlwind, often forgetting half the things I needed to get through my day successfully, like my glasses, wallet, phone and so on. I would suffer for the day because I always felt like I was starting on the back foot. So hectic and so frantic. But that was normal for me – the increased heart rate, feelings of overwhelming stress and playing catch-up. I lived in 'fight or flight' mode, and that's how I survived.

Looking back, I can see that my mornings centred around what I did and who I worked for, not who I was.

What do I need before I face the world? How should I set myself up to feel calm and prepared going into my day? What do I need to do to take myself forward every day? These are questions I never asked myself.

I never made time for me before I gave to other people. I was rushing out the door to please, with no consideration for what I needed to do first. And this is part of the reason that I revolved for so many years.

It's taken me quite some time to find a morning routine that really works for me. Now, mornings are a crucial part of my overall health and one of the reasons I have managed to build a successful business. Because before I give to everyone around me, I set myself up for a good day first. I start every day with a check-in, even if it's just for thirty seconds. Then I know what I need to do in order to give my best self to the world.

My non-negotiables in the morning

Gratitude

The first thing I do when I open my eyes is thank the universe for my life. Every morning when I wake up, I know how lucky I am to face into a day feeling well. When I think about how much I suffered when I was sick, I will never take a normal day for granted again. Because when you've been to hell and back, Mondays don't look so bad any more. Starting my day with gratitude comes naturally now, but at the beginning of my journey I would lie in bed, put my hand on my heart and think of three things I was grateful for. This allowed me to feel gratitude and look for the positive in every day, even when I was feeling very low.

When I was sick at home all day, I had the beautiful scenery around my house to be grateful for. When I couldn't work, I was grateful that I got to spend the day with my baby. When I lost my hair, I could be grateful for my beating heart.

I could see that for every dark cloud there is a silver lining. But we need to take the time to look for it. Once you start a habit of beginning the day with gratitude, it will soon become something you do without even thinking of it. You will feel the overwhelming rush of warmth in your heart, and sometimes that rush of gratitude can take your breath away.

Check-in

The next step for me is to check in with how I am feeling. This is a vital step for my overall wellness. These are the questions that I never considered for so many years:

- What do I need today?

- Am I feeling well or am I feeling low?
- What healthy habit do I need to turn to today?
  - Is it water?
  - Is it good food?
  - Is it time in nature?
  - Is it exercise?

I allow space for my gut feelings, to find what I am trying to tell myself today. My gut feelings are guiding me and giving information to my brain. It's important for me to connect with those feelings because they are messages that I need to hear. This self-awareness helps me grow every day.

Meditation

Before anyone wakes in my house, I start my day with a very short meditation, which usually takes five to seven minutes. This helps give my life perspective. Something will always come up for me in my meditation that helps me see the bigger picture more clearly. If I have a work issue on my mind or something I am worried about, that few minutes of calm in the morning gives me time and space to work through it, to acknowledge it and find a way to move forward. It allows me to process and find solutions. Meditation allows space for guidance and an inner knowing to come through, and usually I know what I need to do afterwards. Meditation prevents me from getting caught up in my day before it's even begun. It is the five minutes of my day that makes the other twenty-three hours and fifty-five minutes better.

It took me a while to find the type of meditation I enjoy, and for me, it's always a guided meditation. I allow my teacher to plant seeds and I enjoy feeling held for those few minutes. Some of my friends enjoy mantra meditation, where you sit and chant. It may take some time to find the right kind of meditation for you, but when you do, you'll soon discover you can't live without this precious gift.

Nourishment

Breakfast at my desk is a thing of the past and a massive NO for me. When I eat on the go or while I'm working, I feel like I am denying myself. Before, my story was 'I have no time'. Now, I make time. Nobody is going to give you time for yourself but *you*. I make time for breakfast. I know that if I go out to work without nourishing myself first, I will suffer. Not only that, but I won't feel well. Breakfast is the key to setting myself up for a good day. I start my morning with a probiotic and afterwards I have oats and fruit. I try to drink a glass of water first thing to hydrate. This way I know I am giving myself the best start and best chance of being my best self.

＊

Things I turn to if I'm feeling low

If I am feeling low, the first thing I do is I try to change my energy. That's my first port of call. I have four tools I use to do this: music, air, nature and affirmations.

Music

I turn on my high-vibrational music, a song that's going to make me feel good or put a pep in my step. During a particularly difficult few months at the end of 2021, I listened to Alex Aiono's 'Good Morning' every morning. I often wondered what my neighbours thought when they would hear the same song playing in my kitchen every day. The lyrics help me face the world and find the good in each day. I couldn't listen to music when I was sick – it was very triggering for me. It reminded me of better days and made me feel so sad. I am happy to report that music has made a big comeback in my life and is now one of my tools to change up my energy.

Find a song that lifts you up and watch the effect it has, not only on you, but on people around you. Good music can lift us higher. Good vibes are contagious. One of the greatest things we've bought for our house is a smart speaker. Now we have any song at our fingertips. That speaker, that one small addition to our home, has brought endless moments of joy to our family. I've gone from turning off radios everywhere I went to dancing around my kitchen to Macklemore on a Monday morning. Never underestimate the power of music and where it can take you.

My high-vibrational playlist

- Alex Aiono – 'Good Morning'
- Lizzo – 'About Damn Time'
- Macklemore feat. Skylar Grey – 'Glorious'
- Macklemore – 'Downtown'
- Groove Armada – 'But I Feel Good'
- Sia – 'Unstoppable'
- Coldplay – 'Higher Power'
- Coldplay – 'Hymn for the Weekend'

Air

I open all the windows in my house. This is key for changing my energy. If I want to shift my low mood, I have to feel like I am letting it out. As they say, out with the old, in with the new. I invite new, fresh air into my house. I let the curtains blow in the wind, and I put on some extra layers if I'm cold.

By keeping all my doors and windows closed, I feel stuck, stagnant, with a lack of forward momentum. By opening the windows, I am letting that low, heavy energy out and inviting the new energy in. That brings hope, that brings life and that brings the new. It is literally a fresh start. Try it!

Nature

Taking myself for a walk in nature in my local forest or by the sea helps me find perspective and self-compassion. When I am in nature, I feel part of the *bigger picture*, because nature is where we came from, nature is home. It gives me space to acknowledge how I am feeling, it gives me an opportunity to be my own cheerleader and it gives me a sense of belonging. I struggle to find this perspective elsewhere. If you don't have a garden, or a park or beach close by, just getting outside to feel the sun on your face and to hear birdsong will do you good. Even watching a nature documentary can create a similar sense of perspective. Nature helps me look at my life from the outside in and can completely transform my day.

Affirmations

When I am really struggling, affirmations can pull me out of a dark hole. I have many that I turn to at different times. At one point in 2019, I was going through a tough time and felt like there was nowhere to turn, so I would sit on my floor and read affirmations over and over again. Slowly, as the days passed, I felt more and more positive and felt a sense of taking myself forward. I emerged from that dark place with an inner knowing that I can get myself through a tough time once I support and love myself during it.

Here are some of my current favourites:

- *I choose not to live in fear* (when I'm getting into the sea)
- *I surrender to creative solutions* (when I have a work issue)
- *I am enough, I have enough, I do enough* (when I'm taking time off or resting)
- *I can, I am and I will* (when I need self-belief)
- *I have a right to change my mind about who I am* (when I'm challenging myself)

*

Things that make my mornings brighter

These are the things that I don't do *every day* but they always make me feel better when I do.

Exercise

If I am feeling well in the morning, there is no stopping me from getting out there and going for a short jog first thing. Experiencing the calm of the outdoors, before the roads get busy, is a joy to me. If I can start my day with exercise, I know I will be flying high for the rest of the day.

Journalling

We all have a lot to do in the mornings, but if I can get a few words down on paper, it helps me excel. Writing things down helps me clear the path for the rest of the day. When I created *The Good Glow Journal*, I wanted to make a space where you can go to evaluate what you really need for the day ahead. It was also important for me to encourage you to connect with what makes you feel well, so you can do more of it. The magic of our journal is that it allows you to assess what you need from a personal point of view first, so that you can excel in your professional life.

If you don't have a journal, a piece of paper can work just as well. You can bring some of the affirmations from p.83 to your journalling practice. So at the top of the page, above your 'to do' list, think about a feeling that you would like to lean into today. It can be something aspirational like wanting to achieve your dreams, or something more grounding like simply reminding yourself that you are loved. Creating an affirmation just for you is a powerful way to start the day. Think of it as your motto or superpower for the day ahead.

Remember there is no right or wrong way to journal. It's about reminding yourself that our brains are not computers, they can become overloaded. By writing things down, you are simply taking the pressure off. It's like clearing your brain of all the clutter.

Embrace
Curiosity

STEP ● ● ❸ ● ●

"

Don't count yourself
out of knowing more.

"

There was a knock on my door during chemotherapy and when I opened it I saw my friend Claire Solan standing on my doorstep. My long-lost friend Claire Solan.

Claire and I used to work the Saturday shift together in Spin. She was a DJ/presenter and I was her newsreader and we loved each other's company. We would spend our Saturdays ordering pizza, cracking jokes – it was always just so easy with her.

We'd often find ourselves still chatting long after our shifts ended. We just made sense together. Now I can see that we were soul sisters long before we knew it.

Before long, Claire landed a big job. She and Aidan Power were to present the breakfast show on 98FM. It was a big deal. I was so delighted for her, because she has such talent. She went off to 98FM and we drifted apart – still friendly with each other but not making that quality time like before.

A couple of years later, Claire's stint on the show came to an end. Soon she decided to move to London, and we lost touch over that time.

When I got sick she sent me a text, and just after I started chemotherapy, while on a trip to Dublin, she asked me if she could call over. I was a bit nervous to see her. I was nervous to see anyone around that time! I had my really close circle around me, but most people were just leaving me to it – I suppose they were giving me space. Meanwhile, Claire was knocking on my door.

When she texted, I did hesitate and considered telling her I wasn't up to it, but something inside was telling me to let her in.

In her beautifully calm way, Claire walked into my house that day and sat down with Jamie, Pia and me. Like a ray of sunshine coming through the door.

I didn't tell her at the time, but I was nervous to see her because something had been on my mind for a couple of years. Her going-away party. Back when she was moving to London (a couple of years before I got sick), she held a going-away party at a bar in town. I remember seeing the invite at the time and doing absolutely nothing about it. I didn't text her back and I didn't show up. And not because I didn't care – I did! It was more that when I was unable to be present in anything, things would just slip by without me noticing. But when I noticed that I hadn't been there for her, the decision ate away at me for years. I remember feeling so guilty for not even saying goodbye to her. How could I be such a bad friend?

This very small decision caused me a great deal of anxiety. Instead of facing Claire and apologising, I just completely avoided her for years! I couldn't face the guilt. I ran from it, because I couldn't cope with the way it made me feel. I told one person, my friend Brendan. He was still in touch with Claire and spoke to her all the time. Every time I brought it up he would say 'Just text her' or 'I can't believe you're still talking about this all these years later'. But I couldn't face it.

Those feelings of guilt and shame would pop up at random moments – when I was doing the dishes or in the shower. They were the soundtrack just playing beneath the surface, around and around: 'You are such a bad friend, how could you not show up, you don't deserve to have any friends …' I was constantly beating myself up, and instead of becoming aware of the impact this was having on me and facing it, I buried it. I pushed it down, further and further. Because that's how I was used to dealing with things. I was full of fear and shame and I held onto those feelings and let them eat away at me.

I promised myself that I would text her. I would! Someday, I would text her and explain! But then I would tell myself that now isn't the right time. And then I would push those feelings down until the next time I thought about Claire Solan.

So all these years later, in 2018, here she was sitting in my rock-bottom moment with me.

That day, I finally got to say I was sorry for not showing up for her and thank her for showing up for me.

As Claire left my house a few hours later, she pressed a package into my hands with such care and intention that I knew it was special. In that package were two books. The first was Oprah's *What I Know for Sure* and the second was Gabby Bernstein's *The Universe Has Your Back*. Claire had come to do a job that day. She'd got a message and followed her heart. And as uncomfortable as she may have been to enter our precious space, she did what her heart told her to do. (This is your sign to knock on the door – if you feel it, do it.)

Claire had gone to London in such pain, but her discovery of self-love, compassion and healing was making not only her world brighter, but mine too. I was sorry to see her go.

I will admit, as she bounced down the steps and I closed my front door, I looked down at my new books and thought, *Who the jaysus is Gabby Bernstein?* But that day two soul sisters came together. Claire got a whisper to come visit me, and I got a whisper to let her in. And those two books changed my life forever.

I had been through a lot over those few months. It was February 2018. By that time, I'd had two cancer surgeries and a round of IVF so we could create some embryos for the future. It felt bizarre doing IVF with my seven-month-old baby in my arms. My doctors told me that my ovaries had an 80 per cent chance of surviving the chemotherapy, and I thought they were pretty good odds, but after some consideration we decided to proceed with a round of IVF. It turns out it was one of the best decisions we ever made as we managed to create fifteen embryos. It felt like a miracle in the middle of such uncertainty. I had been prescribed five months of chemotherapy and four weeks of radiotherapy, and I was told I'd have to take a cancer drug for up to five years. Devastatingly, it is not advisable to conceive while on that particular drug, so my entire world had turned further upside-down. Jamie and I really wanted to give Pia a sibling, so to put those dreams on hold was heart-breaking. My dear friend Danielle Garner, who did my hair on my wedding day, had shaved my head on January 4th. In that moment and the months that followed, I was completely and utterly stripped bare. I felt so vulnerable and scared.

But when I fell, l was never alone. Jamie and my family were there to catch me every single time. Those early days of chemotherapy were so difficult.

One night, a Saturday, Jamie practically carried me from the couch to our bed. It was before 9.30 p.m., and I asked him to stay with me until I fell asleep. A wave of grief hit me in that moment like a tsunami – it was overwhelming. I remember sobbing in the darkness, my pillow soaking wet from the tears. Through the tears I could see Jamie's silhouette in the darkness. He was sitting on the end of the bed, head in his hands, crying, and I remember feeling absolutely broken. We both were. Everything was so different to how we'd imagined. That was as bad as I can remember.

But no matter how bad he was feeling, Jamie was there to hold my head above water, even though he was drowning himself. He never left me, mentally or physically. He guided me, held me, never left me to go out with his friends. He did more for me than anyone will ever know or understand.

I would often feel myself slipping into a dark place at night, but before I had a chance to fall, Jamie would notice and help me. Night after night, the same conversation, the same reassurance; he must have been exhausted. But he did it every time like it was the first time. He never got frustrated with me; he never pretended not to notice. He would stay up well into the night reading medical papers and journals, so the next time I had a question or an irrational thought, he was there with the facts to bring me back to the present. But most of all, he was there with love. He helped me put myself first and never made me feel guilty or selfish. He encouraged me to grow and change.

He gave everything to supporting me during my treatment. And I will be forever grateful to him for that. Forever and ever.

After feeling like I was stuck, reliving the same chapter of my life over and over again, all of a sudden the pages of my life started to turn and turn like never before. Everything was evolving so rapidly. It was like all of these incredible breakthroughs were waiting for me, but I had been too afraid to step into the unknown to see them.

That day with Claire was the start of yet another new chapter. I could see that connecting with myself and my inner world was helping me to feel happier and make better decisions. Those books she gave me were about to open up a new world.

A seed of curiosity had been planted the night I watched the Tony Robbins documentary, when he said life happens *for* you. And because I chose to water it, the seed was about to start growing. I opened Oprah's book *What I Know for Sure* in chemotherapy, and it changed my life. It was like Oprah herself was standing beside me, telling me to believe in myself, telling me a new life was waiting for me. I was starting to see that all the times I told myself it was too late for me was simply a delaying tactic and a lack of belief. Now I could see that fear was stopping my growth and it was time for me to change my story. And that is why we should never underestimate the power of planting a seed.

✳

As I moved through my cancer treatment, I was beginning to let go of the stories that I'd been telling myself and the mindsets I'd become used to. I'd already found a new appreciation for being outside. I started to believe I was strong enough to face my cancer treatment, I was embracing silence in a way that would have terrified me before, and a new world was revealing itself to me as a result. As each new day unfolded, I started to get curious like never before.

I have sat on beaches my entire life watching other people have fun in the sea. I would see their joy, excitement building in me every time I watched. And I had a yearning to swim too.

But I always stayed on the shore, watching. After all, that's how I rolled. I was the biggest cheerleader, an excellent observer, the greatest bystander.

Before I began changing the soundtrack to my life, my role was to watch other people do cool things. They did cool things and I counted myself out.

This included watching people in the sea.

Even though every cell in my body wanted to get into the sea, I didn't. Because I told myself I wasn't the *type of person* who gets into the sea. Even though I would sit there yearning to get into the water so I could *feel alive*, I didn't. I stayed safe, stayed still and stayed small. Because fear ruled my life.

I was so afraid of what other people would think of me if I did something different or something they were not used to me doing. So instead, I did nothing at all. I couldn't see that I was able to step out of the box I had put myself in. That I just had to do something different in order to change. To evolve. So everything stayed the same, and I stayed within the strict boundaries I had set for myself.

There's a story about a man who was passing a group of elephants who were tied to a fence by a very small rope. The man was confused because it was clear that if the elephants wanted to break free, they could easily do so. He saw a trainer close by and asked him why the elephants didn't escape. The trainer explained that from a very young age the elephants were tied to the fence with the rope. And as they grew bigger and bigger they never tried to break free, simply because they believed they still couldn't.

Are you an elephant tied to a fence? What stories have you been telling yourself that are not true? What is your heart telling you to do that your head won't allow? Is it tennis, paddleboarding, boxing? Do you look at a big group of people on the beach tucking into their flasks of tea after a sunrise swim and feel that pang, like you should be doing that too?

How does it feel to be on the outside looking in? Does your heart long to be a part of something bigger? Something meaningful? Something fun?

I am here to tell you that it's OK to step into a new version of yourself. It's OK to let yourself feel joy. Because we aren't born to *stand on the shore*.

During my recovery, one of my best friends, Rebecca, was getting married in Portugal. I had a little break between chemotherapy and radiotherapy, and her wedding was at that perfect time. I was nervous to go, but I couldn't miss it, so Jamie and I flew over with our friends Audrey and Jack. It was the best decision because we were laughing from the minute we arrived at the airport. As much as I needed nutrition, water and exercise, at that time I needed joy and fun too. It was time to start living again and nobody on this earth makes me laugh like Audrey does. I always say God didn't give me a sister, but he gave me Audrey.

One morning as we sat in sunny Portugal, I announced to Jamie, Audrey and Jack that I wanted to get into the sea over the next couple of days, and I asked them all to help me do it. Here I was saying something vulnerable and scary out loud, and their reaction was nothing but support, love and encouragement. Nobody made me feel silly. Nobody made me feel stupid or less than.

So the morning after Becca and Mikey's beautiful wedding, Jack led the way. He marched us through the town of Carvoeiro with a towel tucked under his arm. Everywhere we went, we bumped into people from the wedding. But Jack kept marching on, a man on a mission. As we approached the beach, I said I would prefer if we found a quieter spot further down, because I wanted to take off my wig and I didn't want to make a fuss.

We walked down a bit, then Jamie and Jack jumped straight into the water. The sea was quite wild that day – I remember thinking it was one of the scariest things I'd ever seen, with the waves crashing in and the roar of the water. It was loud and intimidating.

Jamie and Jack were calling us in, so I took off my wig, dropped it onto my towel, held hands with Audrey and ran towards the water.

I will never forget what happened next. Audrey, in the way only Audrey can, started screaming as we were running. She completely let go and let something bigger take over. All I wanted was for this to be a low-key moment in my life but I had no option but to just … live it.

Before I knew it, I was joining in, screaming at the top of my voice, and we jumped into the water. I felt so many emotions all at once. The water crashing against our bodies, over our heads. All of us swimming together and living in the moment. We laughed, I cried, it was unforgettable. I had never felt love and support like it. I felt such a sense of belonging.

And then it hit me, this is JOY!

And I knew joy – I feel it all the time when I look at Pia. But this joy was different. This was joy bubbling up from within. From *inside of me*. I was creating it. It was a moment in time I will never forget, a five-star moment. I closed my eyes and savoured every second. Feeling my feet in the sand at the bottom of the sea, plugged into the earth with the water crashing over my body. I have never felt so alive.

As I walked out of the sea, it was all so clear.

I did it. With a little vulnerability to ask for help, I had just done something I'd told myself I could never do. I had replaced fear with joy by listening to the whispers and finally surrendering to what my heart was telling me to do. I had honoured my feelings and here I was feeling more powerful than I had ever felt in my life.

For the rest of the day, joy followed us around. We laughed, we sang, we hugged, we kissed. It was one of the most unforgettable days of my life because, after all those years, I was finally living.

As we travelled home, I felt like I had been supercharged. I was flying high, operating at a different frequency. I was going home a different mother. I could see now that my biggest fear was my cancer and I'd survived. And I'd always feared the sea and I'd survived that too.

So I started to think, *What else can I survive? What else am I capable of? What more can I do?*

On that trip, I realised that I was just like every person I have ever looked up to and admired. I was capable of the same things and worthy of my own dreams. I was a person who deserved her place in this world. I was free to finally be me.

I had choices, each and every day. I had found a new path and I knew I would never go back to the way things were. All it took was one step forward, one leap of faith. And each new step was revealing the true me. That's all it took. Forward.

That day was my rebirth.

Ever since that weekend in Portugal with my best friends, I have walked a little taller because I found the joy within me. I could see that I am capable of feeling joy, bringing joy to the world because I *am* joy. *Joy doesn't have to happen to me, I can create it.*

Five-star moments

I now look for five-star moments everywhere I go. A five-star moment is a moment in time that feels perfect in every way and brings a sprinkle of joy to your heart and soul. A five-star moment could be a walk on the seafront, the taste of the perfect slice of pizza, an uplifting smile from a stranger – anything that brings you joy, even if it's only for a split second.

When I first spoke about five-star moments on my podcast, my emails and messages exploded. Five-star moments were everywhere. People who follow me started to tag me in all of their five-star moments.

And the more I saw, the more I couldn't believe how similar everyone's five-star moments were. Week after week I was sent so many photos of blue skies, a coastline, a beautiful forest, a moment in the garden with a cup of tea. How often do we speed through life not appreciating the magic in every day? It could be the look of love from your child or partner, a beautiful sky, a thank you to your barista in the morning. These are moments that often slip by without noticing, without thought, without gratitude. If I could give you one piece of advice, it would be to slow down and see all the joy in your life and give thanks for it.

When I sat in a tiny room in Beaumont Hospital being told I had cancer, nothing mattered but the people I loved and the moments I had lived with them. Every laugh, every tear, every hug, every smile. It all became so precious. The joy of life. The joy of Monday mornings, and the joy of five o'clock on a Friday. Every moment is precious and every moment is a gift if we choose to see it that way.

Go look for your five-star moments. Feel them, live them, cherish them.

Now if I ever feel like I'm drowning in life, like things are getting too much, I make my way to the sea. The fear is still there. At times it still has me frozen on the shore. And then I have to start the pep talk and repeat the affirmation:

I choose not to live in fear.
I choose not to live in fear.
I choose not to live in fear.

Then five, four, three, two, one ... I put one foot in front of the other until I get to the water and then I take the leap. Fear, fear, fear, there it is ... and soon it turns to joy, joy, joy. Every single time I make my way out of the water, I'm a little bit closer to the real me. I cannot believe how far I've come.

The sea clears my path so I can be guided in the right direction. The sea helps me find the answers. The sea is my way forward. The sea is a reminder that it's never too late to change your mind about who you are.

✳

I spoke to Gerry Hussey on my podcast about why we live within our comfort zones and tell ourselves stories that create limiting beliefs. He put it so well in his reply.

'As we grow and change, and we are growing every second of every day, nothing is static. So we are never the same person. But the problem is that we hang on to a version of ourselves that no longer exists. A version that we think people will accept or love. And as we begin to grow out of that, when we no longer want to be the problem-solver or the people-pleaser, we are so afraid of not being loved. So our human ego is constantly trying to trap us within the limits of its expectations, and the limits of other people's expectations. But can you give yourself the total freedom to be who you are without judgement, without resistance and without the need to fit into other people's expectations? Can you recreate yourself every day to allow yourself to live from a place of truth, rather than trying to live in this stagnated concept of who we should be? We have to dissolve the ego. Because the ego is the part of the self that is always terrified. The ego says, *What if I'm not enough? What if I'm not seen? What if I'm not respected?* The good news is that we can dissolve the ego through meditation, through prayer, through silence. And then we can begin to see that this thing that we call life is just a transient moment where we get to witness as much love and beauty as we can. And if your intent is to wake up every morning and witness as much beauty and love as possible, you will live an extraordinary life.'

Limiting belief challenge

Is it time to take a look at your limiting beliefs and identify what stories are keeping you safe? What stories are preventing you from living the life you want? It can be helpful to identify them and set an intention so you can move forward.

Grab a piece of paper and write down answers to the below questions:

1. *Without anything and anyone holding me back, what are the things I want to start doing more of?* Create a list of things that you may not have considered doing before – for example, taking up sea swimming, writing a book, going on a solo holiday.

2. *What feelings do you notice when you see yourself as this person?*

3. *What is stopping you from doing these things?* (Be as honest as you can here.)

4. *Can you set an intention around the things you want to start doing more of?* When I want to introduce positive change or I want to change my story, I simply create a new intention. So if your intention is to start sea swimming, can you turn your shower to cold next time? If your intention is to write a book, can you join a book club? If your intention is to go on a solo holiday, can you take yourself out for a solo lunch tomorrow?

Think about the tiny steps and the tiny adjustments you can start making now to help bring you closer to your overall goal. All of these small achievements will help you see that you're limiting beliefs have no power. Try to do something every day that will help you move forward, even if it's something tiny.

Five steps to put you on a path of growth

1 Take a look at your beliefs

The best decision I ever made was to change my mind about who I was. For all of those years when I felt stuck, if I had known how easy it would be, I would have done it much sooner. Try to bring the stories you tell yourself into your conscious mind so that you see them clearly. Often the beliefs we have about ourselves are not true, but we are so used to telling ourselves the same stories day after day that we forget that change is even possible. I soon realised that I wasn't born hating exercise, and I wasn't born with a dislike for the outdoors.

These were stories I'd picked up along the way and attached to my personality. I really and truly believed them. It was only when I stopped and brought those stories into my conscious mind that I was able to see them for what they were: ridiculous and absolutely untrue.

2 Challenge your beliefs

Sometimes we're conditioned to think a certain way about experiences like an illness, a relationship breakdown or a job loss. And we often label these experiences as either 'good' or 'bad'. But when we label things, we can stop them revealing all they are meant to reveal. When I stopped believing that cancer was the 'worst thing' that had ever happened to me, I could see clearly all that it was bringing to my life. We also may have certain beliefs about our bodies, like 'I'm too weak to exercise' or 'I'm too unfit to move'. Or we might tell ourselves we are not morning people. When we do this, we are preventing ourselves from having experiences that could be incredible for us. So can you stop telling yourself you are a certain way?

The next time something goes wrong, ask yourself:

What if this is not the end?

What if this is the start of something new?

What if I am being brought to a place greater than I could have imagined?

What is this experience here to show me?

What is this going to teach everyone around me?

What purpose is this going to bring to my life?

What is this going to help me see differently?

What is this going to help me do?

We spend our lives trying to avoid the pain, the failure, the end of things. And even though life can get messy and uncomfortable at those times, those low points could be showing us a different path, a better way! Because in those dark rock-bottom moments, we can be cracked open and, I promise, through those cracks the light appears.

So that's what we need to see when we are in the depths of a dark place. Even if you can't see why this is happening to you, trust that someday this experience will reveal all that it is supposed to. On those long afternoons during treatment, I would stare at a clock in my kitchen – often sitting in complete silence, just watching the little second hand. *Tick, tick, tick.* Always moving forward. And as I sat there, I thought, *My life is moving forward too*, and I reminded myself that I wouldn't feel like this forever. The clock gave me hope that better days were coming. When I felt myself dipping, when I was losing trust in the journey or feeling impatient, I would just look at the clock. And there it was, my inner knowing, telling me that everything was going to be OK.

In those afternoons, I crossed into a new world. I was open to receiving and open to learning. My new-found curiosity made me lighter. And one of the most powerful messages I received through reading at that time was from Oprah, who in her bestselling book *What I Know for Sure* said, 'anything can be a miracle, a blessing, an opportunity if you choose to see it that way'.

I started to challenge a lot of the stories I had been telling myself since I was a young child. I saw that very early in my life I had decided who I was, what I liked, what I didn't like, what I could do, what I couldn't do. I believed these stories so deeply that life was slipping by and I was counting myself out of so much. It was time to rewrite my story, and you can do it too.

This is your reminder that each day is a new opportunity to become who you want to be. Each day is a new opportunity to step out of old beliefs and old ways. And you can do that by simply doing one thing every day that embodies the type of person you want to become. If you want to evolve and start living the life of your dreams, start today.

Do you want to be healthier? Eat one extra portion of fruit today.

Do you want to be fitter? Move for ten minutes today.

Do you want to feel less stressed? Meditate for five minutes today.

Do you want to feel calm? Breathe deeply for three minutes today.

> Do you feel overwhelmed? Write things down.
> Do you feel a lack of presence? Put down your phone.

When you start living and acting like the person you want to become, your life will start to change. But first you need to show yourself and the universe that you are taking those steps forward. I wasted ten years *waiting* for someone to tap me on my shoulder, to give me a new job, so that I could start living. I spent my life frozen, because I was so afraid to fail. I kept saying, 'I'll be happier when …' 'I'll be healthier when …' So I waited and waited. I told myself, 'Someday it will happen for me – someday I'll show people what I'm made of.'

But no one is coming to tap you on the shoulder. Nobody is going to make it happen for you, but you. So what can you do *today* to start aligning your behaviour with who you want to be?

All it takes is to do something, anything, differently. When you do that, even if it's for one minute, you are taking steps forward. All of a sudden you've taken something positive from a meditation and it's helped you solve that problem that's been hanging over you. Or you run around the block and you realise that you can do hard things. Now you've sparked self-belief. And I promise, that's when things will start happening for you in your external world, because the energy you are putting out there is different.

That's when people start to notice, that's when the new opportunities come your way.

One of my biggest challenges in my recovery was exercise. It was my greatest limiting belief. I never had faith in my body – I always felt weak. But when my oncologist, Professor Jenny Westrup, sat me down in my recovery and said, 'Georgie, you have to exercise,' I knew I had to listen.

Right after chemotherapy, I joined a little gym close to my house. I tried every class and every machine, praying something would click for me. One day, I jumped on a treadmill and said, 'I'll just see if I can run for one kilometre ...' and I could. I'll never forget that day. It was so sunny that I could see my reflection in the glass. My hair had started to come back, I had a trace of eyebrows again, and I had just run for one kilometre. Holy moly. I was excited to go back (well, as excited as you can get about a gym session), and I did it again and again. After two months, I was running for five kilometres. I couldn't believe it. Who was this person? I couldn't believe that after thirty-three years of telling myself I hated something, I was enjoying it. My mind was blown. All of these things in life I'd told myself I hated – exercise, cold weather, being outside. But with just an ounce of curiosity and self-belief, I was breaking free of all those stories that had kept me small for so long. So my stories started to change. Just like that. I do like exercise, I do like fresh air, I love nature!

Before I knew it, I was doing the Parkrun every Saturday, feeling strong and loving life. I was rebuilding my life with new stories. Before long, people close to me started to say, 'Wow, Georgie, you are *glowing*.' And I believed them, because I could see it myself. I looked completely different.

My journey has never been about changing how I looked, but I had started to glow from the inside out. I looked so healthy, my skin was clear, my eyes were bright. For months leading up to my diagnosis I didn't recognise myself because I looked so unwell. In just one year, I had completely transformed not only how I looked on the outside but, most importantly, how I felt on the inside. The change came from within.

Everything and anything became a possibility because I finally loved myself enough to take one tiny step forward every day. And the small changes add up.

The most important thing to remember is to do one small thing every day. A smoothie on Monday, an early night on Tuesday, a meditation on Wednesday, a run around the block on Thursday, a date night (solo or with your partner) on Friday, a swim on Saturday morning, meal prep on Sunday. It all starts to add up, and by giving back to yourself in this way, you start to become important to yourself. And when you become important to yourself, other people start to take notice.

3 Don't try so hard to control the future

One of the greatest things you will ever do for yourself is let go of outcomes. To be honest, I spent my life trying to predict my future, and if you do that yourself, you'll know it's utterly exhausting to live that way.

When you are constantly trying to predict, it is hard to connect with and enjoy the present moment. And the ironic thing is that the present moment is creating your future. When I was sick, I had no expectations of how my day would go. I began to live for the first time in the present. I started to see that, for many years, I had let expectations control my life. And we think these expectations will help us stay on track and create our dreams. But expectations can block our true paths.

When I was forced to stop, I started to feel freer than I'd ever felt. And then I had time and space to get on my own team. To make my life work for me, not against me. For the first time, I wasn't punishing or judging myself. I was very accepting of where life had taken me. For the first time, I was connected with what I needed and giving it to myself. I finally loved myself enough.

I spent so many years trying to get ahead that I had no time to wonder. I believed I had no time for anything else. So I never opened my mind to new concepts, new thoughts or new challenges. All of that stuff was for another day, when I'd made it. But now I can see I was never going to 'make it' because I was never willing to accept that there could be another way.

I believed in one goal, one focus, one path. I believed it with every part of me. I believed it so much that I got stuck there. And I couldn't see that there was more. There was so much more.

What could have been different if I had allowed myself to be open to *something else*? What could have been different if I'd just read one page of a book every morning? What if I'd opened myself up to more? Instead I existed for the weekends or a two-week holiday once a year, hanging in there, surviving until the next payday. I was just another person whose life was working against them, and all I could do was survive another day.

Sometimes we let the business of life take us away from our true selves and dim our lights. We let it take away our dreams and ambitions, our sense of fun or adventure. When we neglect the things that bring us peace and joy, soon enough it becomes normal to live that way. We forget that it is OK to connect with those things.

For years I knew that I needed to change something in my life but I didn't know exactly what that was.

It was only by getting curious, by opening my mind, all while connecting to and listening to myself, that I was able to find what it was that made me whole.

One of the most insightful comments on achieving a sense of happiness and fulfilment I've heard is from Matthew Kelly, author of *Resisting Happiness*. He says that yes, we all want to be happy. We know the things that make us happy but we seem to be too busy to actually do the things that make us happy. Why? Because we're too busy *trying* to be happy!

During treatment, I spent every Monday in hospital. I went from eating breakfast and lunch at my desk every day to eating breakfast and lunch off a hospital tray in an oncology ward. I liked to go to chemotherapy alone because I had a lot to do. I was all of a sudden very curious to discover more about myself and the world, and I needed this space to explore. Now I can see that it was growth day. (Can you schedule some growth days into your calendar?)

Pia was turning one at the time so things were really busy at home, and it was my opportunity to escape into my own world. Once I knew that Pia was safe with my mum at home, I could give Mondays my all. One of those mornings in hospital, tucked up under a blanket, I opened Oprah's book and walked into a new world. I read those nuggets of wisdom, held the book close to my heart and cried. Every second of my life was changing through her words. She was showing me how to love myself, how to live with joy, gratitude, purpose, meaning, self-worth. It was blowing my mind. She was and is my greatest teacher and I was finally ready to listen. My nurse, Grace, would check on me, often seeing the tears. She was so loving – she could see the journey unfolding. And each time another bag of chemotherapy emptied into my body, I stood up and walked out of the hospital a little different. Every second in that chair was helping me to become a better version of myself. Each time I left, I had a little more strength, a lot more knowledge and a little more love for me. Chemotherapy wasn't taking anything from me. Chemotherapy was giving me the opportunity to begin again.

Connect with your paper mothers

While interviewing life coach Martha Beck, who worked with Oprah for twenty years, I asked her about feeling down. I often call it my invisible string. It's like something is pulling me down and I can't quite understand why. Life just feels heavy.

I asked her what we should do if we feel like that in the mornings – if we want to hide under the duvet and avoid the day. And she gave me a way out of this feeling in four simple steps.

1. **Acknowledge the feeling:** First acknowledge that you are not feeling excited for the day ahead.

2. **Let your inner teacher in:** When Martha wants to let her inner teacher in, she turns to her favourite books, or what she likes to call her 'paper mothers' Martha keeps hers right beside her bed. You could do the same.

3. **Read until you find something that makes you feel better:** Keep reading until something clicks with you and makes you feel better.
4. **The knowing:** When you get to the sentence that makes you feel better, know that that is the message you are supposed to hear that day.

Now on the days when I'm feeling low, when the invisible string makes an appearance, I like to explore. It helps me find a way out of the darkness. It could be one page of a book, a walk in nature, a dip in the sea. I do something to change my energy or change my perspective. Because each day is an opportunity to get curious, to grow and learn. To discover something new that will take you forward.

4 Preserve your curiosity (be careful where you put your energy)

We can use our curiosity in lots of different ways. But have you spent your life being curious about all the wrong things? Like with my energy, I was using my curiosity in the wrong places. I was curious about other people, other things, other people's business. But I was never curious about what I could bring to my world outside of work.

What if you could invest your curiosity in yourself? Where might that curiosity take you? What books could you read, or where could you go?

The most important thing to remember is that your life is working for you when you are growing and evolving.

I always considered myself to be curious – after all, I worked in a radio station. The news ruled my life. I felt plugged into what was going on in the world and thrived on 'knowing it all'. I liked being the person that people came to for answers.

During my cancer treatment, I read an interview with Gisele Bündchen, who is a global environmentalist, business woman and supermodel. She says although she cares deeply about the bigger issues of the world, she does not watch the news every day.

I on the other hand was surrounded by it every waking hour for years.

It really made me think, because I always believed that the more you knew, the smarter you were. But in 2017, I had taken a step back. Yes, I knew what was going on in the news, but it wasn't consuming me like before.

I realised that I had never really stepped back before and thought about protecting my own space and energy.

When I worked in the newsroom, it was my job to find the worst news possible and tell people about it.

Of course, there was good news stories too, but they were few and far between.

So can we find balance? Of course, we need to stay connected to the issues in the world, it's a fundamental part of being human and caring for other people, but if the news is on constant refresh is it affecting our mental health?

And this can filter right down to our own homes, within our neighbourhoods, and in our workplaces. Are you so busy being consumed by what everyone else is doing with their lives, that you have no time to grow your own? Can you keep some of your time for your own curiosity and growth?

5 Create some healthy habits

When I had more of a focus on my inner world I was able to connect with myself in a different way. My new-found awareness and presence was helping me to slow down and be more mindful about every decision.

We sometimes forget that choices are all around us and what we choose shapes our life. Our days are filled with choices. That's a lot of choices. And we make most of them without thinking. We walk to work the same way, we might take the lift every day without considering that we could take the stairs, we have a coffee at 3 p.m. because that's what we always do. We are caught up in this cycle of living our lives on autopilot, forgetting there is so much choice everywhere we turn.

My message has never been about enormous change – it is not about overhauling your life in one go. It's how one small decision at a time can take you forward.

My first small decision on my journey was to drink more water. One glass of water at a time. It was a couple of days after I'd found the lump in my breast and I felt so out of control. At that point, I still didn't know if I had cancer or not. But I did know one thing for sure: I was completely and utterly dehydrated. So every morning when I woke up, I trained myself to drink a glass of water before my morning coffee. After a number of weeks, I was drinking more water each day. One mindful glass at a time. In fact, when I started doing this I realised just how thirsty I really was. Sometimes I think I didn't drink water because it was too much of an inconvenience to pee! So I decided to let the water into my life, and it became my first healthy habit. I wasn't even familiar with the term 'healthy habits' back then. I was just getting on with it.

Sure enough, the water had a knock-on effect. A couple of months later, I decided to give myself a target of five to seven portions of fruit and vegetables a day. It's important to note that I never gave anything up (except for processed meat and fizzy drinks) when I got sick. All I did was start adding healthier foods into my day. And after a couple of weeks of being mindful of what I was putting into my body, it just became a normal part of my day. My plate was becoming more colourful and so was my life.

Once I had that healthy habit under my belt, I started exercising.

All I did was take one healthy habit at a time. I gave each habit plenty of space before I looked to the next – I worked on one for a couple of months, and when it became second nature to drink more water, to eat more fruit and veg, then I was ready for another. The vital thing for me was that I didn't try to do it all at once. I knew I needed lasting change, and if I did everything at the same time, it would never have lasted.

Day by day, step by step, one decision at a time, is the key to real change. Now I try to take on two or three new healthy habits per year. And with each year, I am discovering more and more about myself. I rebuilt my life with new stories and new ambitions. And now, I believe I am capable of anything.

A moment to pause

So, let's finish this step with a little reflection, asking yourself these questions and resting in the space of what you notice:

Where can I bring more curiosity into my life?

What new things can I try this week?

What decisions can I look at with a new perspective?

And always remember, there's a whole world of possibilities out there waiting for you to explore.

"

When I embrace joy,
everything in my life
falls into place. I choose
joy every day.

"

Just One More Thing ...
Seek Joy

Did you know you have the power to hit your joy button whenever you need it?

I was out for a walk one day, listening to Martha Beck on a podcast. It was gold. Everything she said made so much sense. In that moment, I vowed to speak to her on my own podcast. I believed in that moment that I would make it happen, and once I acknowledged the feeling, I had to find a way. So I put a plan into action. I did all I could and then I handed it over to the universe.

We were out for Joe's sixtieth one lovely Sunday. Our entire family was in a restaurant in town – it was such a treat and everybody was in great form. Jamie was a couple of seats down from me, and he reached behind my brother's girlfriend Sophie and tapped me on the shoulder. I looked over at him and he said he'd just got an email from her people. 'Martha's in,' he said.

My opportunity had arrived, and a couple of weeks

later it was finally time to speak to Martha. She was everything I'd imagined her to be. The podcast was filled with so many *aha* moments, but something she said really stuck with me and is now a part of my everyday life.

A big part of Martha's journey is to live with as much joy as possible. She considers joy in everything she does. So I asked her how we can do it too. She thought about it for a second and then asked me if I ever played the game 'it's getting hotter, it's getting colder' as a child. I said yes, I had just been playing it with Pia.

Martha said, 'Well, that's how your true self communicates with you. That's how you get your instructions.' Our inner knowing and what is right for us will feel warm, and what's not right for us will make us feel cold. She explained to me that when it comes to tough decisions, we need to lean towards what is going to make us feel warmer. She says when we choose what feels warmer, we will have a more joyful life.

That really hit home for me that day, and a couple of months later, I got to put it to the test.

I had been nominated for an award – it was a big deal to me. I couldn't believe I was in this category and even considered at an awards show of its kind. I was so flattered and really wanted to go. I immediately started to wonder what I would wear, who I would go with. All of these thoughts were flooding my mind, and before I knew it I had gotten completely carried away with the thoughts of it. Later that day I told my mum, and she reminded me that the awards show was actually on the same day as my cousin's wedding. My cousin Andrea, who had minded me as a child – we were so close growing up, like sisters. I couldn't believe that these two events were falling on the same day. My heart sank. What was I going to do? My head was telling me to go to the awards show and my heart was with the wedding.

I went through every scenario:

Andrea will understand.

I need to focus on my business this year.

I could find some amazing podcast guests at the awards show.

If I don't go, I'll never get nominated again.

I HAVE TO GO.

You can see that I was being taken over by fear. My ego was telling me to go to the awards show, trying to keep me safe. So I decided I had to go to the awards show.

As the days went on, no matter how hard I tried, I just couldn't pick up the phone to tell Andrea I couldn't go to the wedding. It started to weigh heavily on me. I knew I needed to address it – I was driving myself mad – and then I remembered what Martha had told me. I remembered the story about feeling warm and feeling cold.

So I became still. I was going to sit with myself. Instead of zooming through life and making decisions without much thought, I knew a better way.

I started to think about the awards show. Yes, it would be great to go – it's so nice to dress up and walk a red carpet. It would be good for my brand. I wanted to show my appreciation for being nominated. I wanted to show that I cared and that I was grateful. But then what?

I imagined myself sitting down at the ceremony and thinking about Andrea and my family being together, laughing, having a great time. I imagined how I would feel in that moment. When I thought of being away from Andrea's special day, I knew I would feel alone, even though I would be in a room full of people. And I knew I would feel guilty. Definitely guilty. And when I thought of the reality of the situation I started to feel cold.

I moved through that feeling and, in my mind, put myself at the wedding. It would be so great to see everyone. I smiled as I thought about all the laughs we'd have. I'd get to see so many people that I hadn't seen in a long time. People who are important to me. And the memories! We would make memories that would last forever. And I started to feel warm.

I could see then that, as great as the awards show would be for me and *The Good Glow*, my ego wanted me to walk the red carpet, but my heart was with my family.

I slowly opened my eyes and there was the answer.

Weeks later, as I watched Andrea say 'I do' to the love of her life, Dan, I could feel the love, the joy. I looked up at the altar with tears in my eyes, knowing I had made the right decision, and in that moment I was so grateful for all that Martha and this experience had taught me.

So next time you have a tough decision to make, ask yourself what makes you feel warm, free and joyful. Check in with yourself first. Because something will always feel more peaceful. And when you choose that feeling over and over again, your whole life will soon feel very, very warm.

**Slow down
to speed up.**

Lunch Habits

I often wonder how long my mind would have pushed me for if my body hadn't given up in 2017. I just kept going until I eventually fell down. Every day for ten years I worked through my lunch break, never giving myself a rest or a chance to recuperate. The truth is, I felt guilty if I took a break. It felt selfish, like I wasn't giving it my all. So instead of taking time that was meant for me, I would give more of myself to my job. And this is what we have to remember: a break is a chance to pause, to refill, to reset and give back to yourself. Your breaks are among the most important parts of your day. Taking a break is not something you should feel guilty about. In fact, taking a break could speed you up in the long run.

One of the biggest and greatest boundaries I have ever set for myself is no work at lunchtime. I allow myself to pause, re-evaluate and reassess. I am no longer prepared to give everything I have to everything I do. I did that for so many years, and it got me nowhere. So lunch breaks look a little different these days, even if I only take twenty minutes.

When I worked in radio, I never left my desk. That meant lunch was served up right in front of my computer screen, in the same seat where I would sit all day long. I worked as I ate. Thinking back to that time, all the hours in the day were muddled into one giant blur. Leaving my desk was a struggle, so I'd often ask someone in the office to pick me up some lunch. If I did leave the office, I always came back feeling better after some fresh air. The day felt a little brighter in the afternoon, like I had more energy. But you guessed it: I would barely notice the positive effect that had on my life.

Break the cycle of work

So if you struggle to leave the desk, if you keep pushing yourself day after day, say one of the following affirmations to override the work pattern, to stand up and walk away:

- *I love myself enough to take this break.*
- *I am grateful for this time to recharge and reset myself.*
- *When I do less, I make more space for what matters most.*
- *Today, I release the desire to rush. I pause, and I breathe.*
- *I am more effective when I take breaks.*
- *What I do today has the potential to improve all my tomorrows.*

- *I honour my mind and body with rest.*
- *I am taking care of myself by allowing myself to take a break.*

Now that you have broken the work cycle and you have decided to pause, think about NOON at lunchtime:

- **N**o work
- **O**utside
- **O**rganise
- **N**ourishment

No work

The most important aspect of my lunch break is that it needs to look different to the rest of my day.

When I think about all the things I could have used my break for over the years, all those lost hours that I could have been putting back into … me! Now that I value myself more, I can see that life is precious, and we are precious. I can see the importance of taking breaks and I can see that if you do not recharge, you will eventually break down.

Lunchtime is now an opportunity for me to fill myself back up again, to reinvest in myself. It's a pit stop for a few minutes, so I can see where I'm at. It's a chance to ask myself what I need for the rest of the day. Is it more water? Is it some fresh air? What sort of pick-me-up do I need right now?

Outside

Part of my lunchtime routine is to step into nature, even if it's just for five minutes. In the summer, I try to eat outside as much as possible. Allowing myself to breathe in fresh air helps me to reset and refocus for the rest of the day. I sometimes refer to it as 'washing my brain', so if it's windy and wild, even better. I always come back to my desk feeling more positive about my day. It gives me space, perspective and a chance to catch up with myself. I step outside because I know I deserve that couple of minutes of peace.

Organise

Use your lunch break to make that appointment you keep putting off. We go to work or fill our days usually doing things for other people or for the greater good of our family. But what about *you*? Has another week passed where you haven't made an appointment to get your bloods done or have that mole checked? When did you last make time to check your breasts? Or book a smear test? What about cancelling that direct debit you keep meaning to? Do you keep missing the opportunity to go to the bank to open that savings account you've been thinking about starting for years?

Part of my lunch break is now to check in with myself and think about the bigger picture of my life. When we work through our lunch breaks, days turn into months, which eventually turn into years. We go around in circles. We find ourselves starting another new year where everything has stayed the same. Your life won't move along if you do nothing to move it along. So stop, take the break, look at the big picture and use this time to reinvest in yourself.

Nourishment

Lunchtime is a new opportunity for me to stock up on my fruit, veg and water intake. This is time to refuel. I eat big lunches because I know if I skip lunch, the quality of my work for the rest of the day will be poor. It's soup in the winter and salad in the summer for me, along with a big side – either a sandwich, a wrap, houmous and crackers or a smoothie. I try to eat in season as much as I can, so in the winter months I will have hearty, thick vegetable soups, and in the summer I will fill up on spinach, lettuce, tomatoes (often from my garden), cucumber and avocado salads. My lunches are not beige any more – they are full of colour. I also love leftovers and will try to 'cook once, eat twice' as much as I can, especially in the winter. If I have some leftover pasta, I will wash some fresh spinach or kale and throw it on top.

I check the Bord Bia website to see what's in season each month and try to fill my trolley with as much in-season, organic fruit and vegetables as possible. In terms of organic food, I try to buy organic berries, apples, lettuce, tomatoes, peppers and celery – the fruit and veg that I eat whole. When it comes to things I can peel, like bananas, oranges and carrots, I'm not so fussy about choosing organic. Every day when I finish my lunch, I get some mint tea and a piece of dark chocolate and bring that treat back to my desk.

✳

When it's time to work again, first acknowledge that you have done yourself a great service by pausing and taking that break. I usually say, 'I am making progress every day,' and get straight back to it with a fresh mind and often a fresh perspective, knowing that I am doing great things for myself every day.

Create
the Change

STEP ● ● ● ④ ●

"

It is OK for me
to release what does not
bring me peace.

"

In my recovery it felt like I could see everything differently. I was so happy to be alive, to be given a second chance, that I was determined to take it with both hands.

I was given the all-clear to go back to work in October 2018, exactly one year after my diagnosis, and it was my first time back in Dublin city centre after a very long time. Everything felt so different.

The fast pace, how quickly people lost their tempers on the road, everyone was rushing around, it was overwhelming. It was only when I went back to normal life, or what I had thought was normal life, that I could see how different I was. I could see how much I'd changed in those eighteen months at home.

I used to reach boiling point if I missed a green light or if somebody skipped me in a queue. Now I could see that it was all just wasted energy. I was in a place where I wanted to protect my inner world and not let external factors bring me from a place of happiness, peace and gratitude to rage and upset.

I used to hate Mondays. But now, after spending Mondays in hospital each week, I could see that Mondays aren't so bad after all. Actually, Mondays are great, because they give you an opportunity to begin again. In fact, every day is an opportunity to start anew.

I could see how much of life I took for granted when I was well. How privileged was I to think waking up and being well enough to live my life was a pain in the ass!

It's one of the biggest clichés in the world, but life really can change in an instant. And not only does everything change, you don't even get a chance to say goodbye to your old life. One moment it is one way, and the next moment it's the other.

So I vowed in my recovery to be grateful for every new day, every moment of sunshine and every breath. And not only that, I was going to use my second chance for good. I knew that somehow I wanted to show people how lucky we are just to be here.

In the weeks before I went back to the office, I was excited to see my friends, but nervous about having to work in Spin. I felt so removed from the world of entertainment. A week or so before I was due back, my bosses called me and said a job in 98FM had become available and would I like to interview for it. 'What job is it?' I asked eagerly. 'To read the news on the breakfast show,' they replied. OMG this was it! This was my chance to go for it. But straight away the limiting beliefs started knocking.

You'll never get it.

You've been out of the office for eighteen months.

If you didn't get it before, why would you get it now?

But I decided to go for it, and I GOT THE JOB. My dream. After twelve years I'd got the job. I was so happy. This was the fresh start I needed. I tried to make sense of it. Why now? Why after all this time? And then it hit me. *Oh no. They must feel sorry for me. That has to be it*, I thought. *I mean, I'm still in a wig – they're trying to cheer me up. They obviously felt like they had to give it to me.*

But this was a big opportunity and I was going to give it my everything. It was incredible to see my friends Michael, Kim, Brendan, Trish, Susan – they were like my second family. I was excited to get going. But something happened after a few days in my new job and it all became clear.

I could see that I hadn't got the job because they felt sorry for me: I'd got the job because of who *I had become*. I was so different. My inner world was secure and confident. I was full of self-belief. I loved and cared for myself. I was so happy in who I was that I was putting out a different energy into the world.

Sitting there in the same office, eighteen months later, helped me realise just how much I had changed. It was such a stop-in-my-tracks *aha* moment for me. This was the proof that when you concentrate on your inner world, it makes things happen for you in your external world. When you invest in yourself, it not only changes you but it changes the world you live in.

What if, for all of those years in Spin, I'd become less worried about the external and cared more about what was going on inside of me? What if I had kept something for myself at the end of every day? If I had taken the time to check in with myself every morning or helped myself in some way?

I gave so much of myself to my job and the people around me that I had absolutely nothing left for myself. I woke up and ran out my front door every morning, ate breakfast at my desk, never took a lunch break and often worked overtime. Then I would go home to do chores, cook dinner, then collapse on the couch and crawl into bed. When my alarm went off the next morning, I did it all over again. At the weekends I socialised and burned the candle at both ends, going into the next week more depleted than the last. This went on for years, becoming more and more spent and never giving anything back to myself. How did I expect to thrive? And not even thrive, how did I expect to survive?

When we live like this, when do we recover? Where is the space to grow? When do we plan?

Now, what if you decided to keep 1 per cent of your day just for you? What if you decided to give yourself 1 per cent more each day?

Just 1 per cent of your day is less than fifteen minutes. What could be different in those minutes? Could it be a walk around the block, a short meditation, a few pages of a self-help book? Some space to create affirmations that you can repeat to yourself each morning? Imagine all the growing you could do by taking just fifteen minutes per day!

Now think about what your life would be like in one year's time if you gave yourself that 1 per cent? Probably very different to what it looks like if you are used to giving yourself nothing. If a plane takes off from LA to fly directly to Rome, it will take twelve hours to get there. If the same plane takes off from LA and it's pointed one degree to the right, it will end up somewhere completely different in twelve hours. And that's how much a small change can make over a long distance.

When I think back to all those days that I spent going around and around in circles, I wonder what could have been different if I had given myself just 1 per cent more. Where would I have ended up? This is what we need to realise. If we give every part of ourselves and our energy to the external world, it will keep taking and taking until there is nothing left of us.

That was a hard lesson for me to learn. But it was as clear as day. I got the job in 98FM because of all the work I had done within. I could finally see that investing in yourself takes you forward. And, I promise, this will be the greatest investment you will ever make.

＊

Back in the office, every day passed in an instant as I worked on news stories and presented them on air. I kept reminding myself that this was where I had always wanted to be. But after a couple of months, I started to feel very uneasy.

The office politics, eating at my desk again, the horrific news stories about death, drugs and cancer were all getting on top of me. I would feel myself panicking, and often I would lock myself in the bathroom and just put my head in my hands. What was I going to do? Where could I go from there? Everything was dragging me down.

Because I was on the breakfast show, I was getting up at 4.30 every morning and driving into town to start work at 5.30 a.m. I would sit at my desk and read terrible stories about what was going on in the world, and it was my job to wake people up with them. It was the opposite of how I wanted to live.

I had also started to worry about my health again and my lack of sleep. It had only been a year since my diagnosis and I was terrified of relapsing. I started to get overwhelming feelings of doom. I was so worried about myself that I would chop raw carrots every night and eat them on the way to work at 5 a.m. I was becoming depleted again and was desperately trying to put some good back into my body.

I was good at getting out and going for a walk on my break, I was trying to stay well, but my friends at work started to notice my decline. My mum was incredible at this time. She took care of Pia, and every time I came home the washing and ironing were done, and she even stayed while I napped. She's always supporting me in ways which I could never even put into words.

We shared an office with Newstalk and Today FM at the time, and the health and wellness show on Newstalk was presented by one of my great friends, Clare McKenna. I noticed one day that she was away and, to be really honest, I was disappointed I hadn't been asked to cover her or even learn the ropes on the show.

I had been sharing my health and wellness journey online and thought if anything came up in the area I might get a shout. But then it hit me. Here I am again, sitting at my desk expecting the tap on the shoulder! When am I going to learn that nobody is going to hand me the life I want? I needed to make it happen for myself.

So I stopped waiting and started thinking. It was clear I wasn't going to be given a show. So I started to think outside the box.

I remembered the time I shared my story on Today FM, I had just been diagnosed and my friend Susan Keogh was filling in on Matt Cooper's drive-time show. She invited me onto the show and interviewed me. To this day, I am still stopped in the street by people who heard it. But there was one stand-out piece of feedback I received, that I never forgot. It was from a lady called Caroline, I bumped into her a few days later and she said, 'Georgie, I was out for a run listening to your interview, and I had to stop running because my heartbeat was distracting me from what you were saying.'

And so, all these months later, it hit me.

It was such a lightbulb moment.

We want to hear from each other.

Where do women in Ireland go to share their stories?

We are used to ten-minute interview slots on radio and TV. But where can we listen to each other's stories in full?

On TV and radio, it's all so fast. But why?

I wanted to hear longer conversations.

Over the previous year, I had become an ambassador for Breast Cancer Ireland and had shared my story on radio and TV a number of times. When I was being interviewed, I could barely scratch the surface before the time ran out. Everything had to be condensed. And often the important stuff, like the learnings and the positives and the growth, didn't get any airtime.

I thought, *If nobody else is giving women this platform, I will!*

What if I could create a place where women could tell their stories? What if I could create a space where we could learn from each other?

And that's when the idea for a podcast struck me.

That evening, I casually mentioned it to Jamie. I was more nervous to say it out loud than I let on. I just wanted to see his reaction without making a big deal of it. He was making dinner at the time, and I'll never forget what he did when I told him. He stopped in his tracks, looked at me and said, 'That's exactly what you should do.' That was the night *The Good Glow* was born.

I started booking guests on my lunch break, building my website in between bulletins and recording in a studio after work. I had a small audience on Instagram through sharing my story, a loyal supportive community that I was so grateful for. It was time for me to give back to them.

The Good Glow started to connect with people; women were sharing it and telling their friends to listen.

All of a sudden I had a feeling of purpose. I wanted to help women tell their stories. I wanted to give their voices a platform. I wanted to make *The Good Glow* a sacred and safe place where we could encourage, inspire and help guide each other through the ups and downs.

I never started it to make money or set up my own business, and I think that's why it worked. The intention behind it was pure.

After a few episodes, the podcast started to build momentum and people began talking about it in the office. One day a listener sent me a screenshot of my podcast trending on Spotify. I was so shocked – I couldn't believe it. I didn't even know a podcast chart existed.

And while *The Good Glow* was full of positivity and hope, the crying in the bathroom continued, as did the carrots on the N11. I was spiralling in the newsroom and it was becoming too much.

It all came to a head when, one day, I was sitting at my desk and I placed my left hand on my shoulder and felt a big, hard lump. I jumped off my chair and Susan, who sat beside me, thought I had fallen off it. I grabbed her hand and ran with her to an empty studio. Brendan noticed something was very wrong and followed us. I got onto my hands and knees and started crying. 'I've found a lump on my shoulder,' I said through the tears. They looked so shocked. They sat me down on a chair and Susan asked if she could feel it. I couldn't breathe – all I could think about was my baby. I pulled off my top in a panic and sat there in my bra with my friend feeling for lumps. At that moment I thought I was going back. This was it for me.

Susan felt the lump and she looked startled. 'Georgie, that's the end of your collarbone – that's a bone.' Then Brendan felt it and he confirmed that, yes, it was a bone. I looked at them in shock, and I have never felt relief like it in my life.

All of a sudden I felt giddy. I felt like screaming with happiness. I felt like I had just climbed a mountain or finished a marathon. I was crying and then I was laughing. The relief! I felt completely and utterly deranged. I felt like I had lost my mind. I knew I was acting really weird.

They sent me home a few minutes before my shift ended,

and I called Jamie and told him what had happened. He sounded confused and reminded me that the very same thing had happened on the couch a few months before. He seemed shocked that I couldn't remember it.

That was when I knew I was really traumatised from my cancer, and thankfully I had a therapy session booked with Berna that night. She explained to me that sometimes in a panic attack it can be hard to remember things that have happened before, and that's why I couldn't remember what had happened with Jamie.

That day I knew that I was pushing myself too far. I was getting all of these signs, and while before I would have pushed them away and kept going, I had learned the hard way and I was not going to ignore how I felt this time. There was too much at stake.

I had been back to work for seven months, and that summer I applied for five weeks of parental leave, with plans to take a further two weeks from my own leave. My podcast had reached one million downloads. I couldn't believe it. Taking that much time off is something I would have never considered for even a second before, but I needed to get away from the news for a few weeks. I needed to get back to me. Consuming so much news was becoming toxic in my life and it was dragging me down. On the other hand, I had *The Good Glow*, which was so positive and so hopeful. They were so different from each other.

We booked flights to Spain to escape with my mum and Joe. Jamie, Pia and I cherished every second. I needed space to think clearly about what I wanted to do next. Mum and Joe left after a couple of weeks and so it was just the three of us then.

That week I finally picked up *The Universe Has Your Back* by Gabby Bernstein, one of the books Claire Solan had given me when she came to visit. I had tried to read it a couple of times but it just didn't connect. I wasn't ready. But something was telling me that now it was time.

Gabby is a big believer in signs, and halfway through she tells the reader that if they are looking for guidance they should ask for a sign. I was at the pool at the time and thought, *What could my sign be?* I tried really hard but I couldn't think of one so I continued reading.

The next thing Gabby said was 'don't overthink it' – just ask for whatever sign comes into your head. I thought again and the first person that came into my head was Oprah. Maybe she could be my sign? But I talked myself out of it straight away because she felt too obvious. I get DMs and messages about her book *What I Know for Sure* every day because I have spoken about it so much.

So I thought, *OK, I'll narrow it down a little.* Where have I never seen Oprah before? I have never seen Oprah on Netflix. So it was decided, Oprah on Netflix would be my sign – Oprah's face beside the Netflix logo. I told myself that if I got the sign I would quit my job. I felt immediate reassurance that I wouldn't have to actually quit, because I had never seen Oprah on Netflix. Ever!

That night we decided to stay in, and after dinner Jamie popped down to the basement to dispose of the bin. I picked up the remote and decided to go looking for Oprah. I was so certain she wasn't on Netflix that I didn't bother checking there first, I looked for her on Amazon Prime instead. I told myself that if I found her there, then that would be sort of the same thing.

I spent ten minutes scrolling through every film on Amazon, looking for anything that Oprah had starred in. I kept scrolling, but I just couldn't find her.

I could hear Jamie making his way back into the apartment, so in that second I flicked over to Netflix to pick something for us to watch together. As I pressed the Netflix button on the remote, I nearly fell over. There she was on the Netflix home page – a giant picture of Oprah right beside the logo. What was happening? My jaw was on the floor.

Unbeknownst to me, that day an interview Oprah had hosted had been released on the platform and it was being promoted on the home page. I was completely gobsmacked.

Jamie walked into the room, did a double take and asked if I was OK. I looked up at him and all I could muster was a 'yep'. I couldn't begin to explain what had just happened. I hadn't told him about the sign, so I kept it to myself.

I sat there for the whole night, silent with my thoughts. Shook to the core. Knowing what I had to do. I had to quit my job.

I could see that this was the final sign, because, really, I had been getting signs for months. The crying, the carrots, the madness – they were all signs that I needed to make a change. I was finally ready to listen.

The next morning, after sleeping on it, I told Jamie the entire story from start to finish. I told him that I couldn't work in the newsroom any more and that now I had received my sign I had to quit. Luckily, Jamie had a good job, and I knew if we made some adjustments we could get by on one salary. He told me he would support my decision and we would find a way to make it work.

I know that I wreck Jamie's head talking about signs

and the universe, and he definitely thought I was losing it that day. But after our conversation he wanted to test my theory, so he too secretly asked for a sign. He said to himself that if he got it, it would prove that signs were real.

Later that night, as we walked to dinner, he suddenly stopped and looked at me as a car drove past. He then told me he had asked for a sign earlier in the day – a really rare car in an obscure colour. And that exact car in that exact colour had just driven past us.

It was crystal clear to both of us at that point.

It was time to go.

Now whenever I need guidance I ask for a sign, and you can too. Signs can guide us and support us. They can give us a reassuring arm, show us the way.

✳

I came home from that holiday knowing that I was about to do one of the scariest things I've ever done in my life. But at the same time I was about to set myself free.

I arranged a meeting with Lucy Gaffney, the chair of Communicorp, the company that owned the radio station group. She was the top boss in the company and very close to Jamie. When I got sick, she was one of the first people we called. She really looked after me. I was nervous to tell her that I had to leave. I didn't want to seem ungrateful, but she couldn't have been more supportive. She is a big supporter of women and that day she did nothing other than put wind in my sails. I am forever grateful.

Then it was time to break the news at work – I was unsure how it would go down. But when I eventually came out with it, nobody tried to stop me. They just let me go. There were no goodbyes outside of my immediate friends, no party, no drinks, no fuss. Not even a card. I just never went back after my parental leave. The old me would have been devastated, heartbroken even! To leave without a goodbye just felt so weird. I had put so much into that part of my life for twelve years – I loved being part of the team, and it had felt like family for so long. But it was clear, as it should have been from the start, that in a million years it could never have given back to me what I put in.

The most important thing was that I had Lucy's and my close friends' support, and that's all that mattered to me. Going back to the story of the professor with the jar, we need to remember that work is just the pebbles, and we should never let the pebbles take up all the space.

So just like those before me, it was my time to go.

It was different and I was different. I was at peace with that and I was so proud of myself. I was shaking off the things that no longer served me. I could see that going into the newsroom every day was not helping me to grow or evolve. In fact, it was stopping me from becoming who I knew I had the power to be.

For the first time, I felt bigger than my job. For the first time, it felt as though what I did didn't own me. For the first time, I felt like I was present and making active decisions in my life – making decisions based on what was right for me now, instead of being afraid to make decisions in case they harmed me in the future. I was finally stepping up and owning my life. Owning who I wanted to be and where I wanted to go.

It was also not lost on me that I'd only lasted a few months in the job that I had wanted for twelve years. I was so grateful for everything my experience in radio had taught me (and I know the podcast wouldn't be what it is today without it). But now I could see that this job was never meant to be my path. I was proud of the work I had done, but I believed that my energy and gifts were now taking me in a different direction.

And this is a question we can all ask ourselves. Are you wasting your talents? Do you have more to give to the world? Is it time to stop holding yourself back from what you were put here to do?

So many of us want to give, and we think it's right to give, but we need to be mindful of what we are giving to. I was putting 90 per cent of my energy at that time into reading the news. The truth was I didn't even want to hear those stories myself!

By quitting, I was leaning towards what was making me feel warm.

I was at an event with Audrey the day my resignation was formally accepted. I knew it was coming but that afternoon it was finally official. It arrived in my inbox in black and white and it felt so good.

Thirty minutes later, my agent, David, called me. He told me I had landed a contract to work with a brand for a year. They were going to pay me the same amount as my salary in the newsroom!

And I could see then: sometimes you have to close one door before the next one opens.

*

I held myself back from my dreams because they were so big they scared me. They scared me so much I was too afraid to even think about them or admit them to myself. I filled my life with doing, but I never stopped to ask why or what I was actually trying to achieve. But when I really started to value and love myself, everything began to fall into place in my life. I want to give you some tips on how we can change our stories and put ourselves on a path of growth.

Figuring out your 'I am'

Pastor Joel Osteen is a powerful speaker and someone who has made a great impact on me. In this book *The Power of I AM*, he says that whatever follows 'I am' determines what sort of life you will live, and whatever follows 'I am' is going to come looking for you. So we need to be really careful about what 'I am's we choose.

For so long mine were:

I am not good enough.

I am less than.

I am not clever enough.

I am not a real journalist.

I am not worthy of a better job.

I am unseen.

I am unfit.

I am a smoker.

I am weak.

I am not able to cope.

I told myself all these damaging things day in, day out.

Joel says when you say 'I am so tired', tiredness will come looking for you. When you say 'I am so unfit', an unhealthy life will come looking for you. So whatever follows 'I am', you are handing an invitation to exist in your world.

Before, when things didn't go my way, I told myself it was because 'I am' a certain way. Too stupid, too boring, too ugly. Too weak, too unlikable. It went on and on. The beliefs I had about myself held me back time and time again.

These beliefs were the reason why I revolved for so long, because I couldn't break the cycle. And I wasn't even aware of how damaging these stories were. I had become so used to them that they felt normal.

I get asked all the time, 'how do you change without an earthquake, without something going terribly wrong?' People tell me that they *want* to change, but they can't seem to find the motivation.

My answer is always the same: the fact that you are even *curious* about change is the first step.

During treatment my mum would come to my house and we would go out for a walk with Pia. My mum gave me a huge gift during those days and months. She let me think out loud while I was figuring it all out. She was my sounding board – she would nod along, walk with me, listen to my ramblings and let me feel what I was feeling. Never telling me how I should feel. She was there when I needed company but she was also there when I needed space. Like an angel, she always managed to find the perfect balance. I know that took great awareness from her.

She was by my side as I began to see life through a different lens. She knew when to give and she knew when to hold back. I am forever grateful to her for all the thought that must have gone into that.

During treatment, everything had stopped, and for most of the week I no longer had anywhere to be. So for the first time, I got to feature on my 'to do' list. I started to ask myself what I needed and what was going to make me feel better that day.

Something that struck me very early on was that a rock-bottom moment can make you feel disconnected from the rest of the world, as if you are no longer part of normal society. You are different from everyone else. And then you can start to feel removed from the 'everydayness' of life. You remember stressing over silly things like a traffic jam. You miss it sometimes, but at the same time, you don't.

Then on the other side, in a completely different way, a rock-bottom moment connects you to the rest of the world, because it plugs you in – you can see the good in other people more clearly. The compassion, the care. And instead of beeping your horn at someone on the road who's cut in front of you, you wonder what's going on in their world today. You start to see the 'humanness' of it all. You might walk past someone with their head down in the park or on the seafront and feel an overwhelming connection to them, even though you haven't looked at each other. Because now you recognise pain. And you can see it in other people.

On those days, I felt less alone, like it wasn't just me. This path had been paved before me. Other people had walked it. Other people had survived it. And not only survived it, but they had gone on to make a difference. What if that could be my story too?

Pia still napped for two hours every afternoon. Everyone would encourage me to sleep when Pia slept, but I couldn't do that. Because I couldn't face waking up twice in one day. It was too painful. You know that feeling when you wake up in the morning, when everything is OK for just a split second? And then you remember – your heart breaks all over again when you remember your reality? That happened to me every time I opened my eyes. I couldn't take it twice in one day.

So instead of sleeping, I sat. I sat, for the first time in my life, in silence. It was my time to figure it all out. I thought about my friends in those days and how life was continuing as normal for them. It was hard for me to process at times how different it was for me. But the most important thing was not to reject my journey or hate it. So I was willing to let it all in and see where it was taking me.

I ran from silence before, and now I longed for it. Those days gave me a lot of time and space to think.

So back to the big question: how do you actually change? How can we transform our lives? Well, it's taken me a long time to figure it all out, but sitting in silence to let your thoughts in can take you in a completely different direction.

When I sat in silence I finally had the space and the clarity to see that I had had it all wrong for so many years. How had I let it get that far?

I could finally see that all of the things I had been telling myself for so many years were just not true. I was proving myself wrong about so much. I'd always told myself 'I can't cope'. And here I was *coping*.

I was in my garden, outside, and I felt good. But wait, I had told myself that I hated being outside. Now the outside was helping me? That didn't make sense.

I could see that I had opened an imaginary box very early in my life and put myself in it. I had wrapped myself up in all of these untruths about myself and who I thought I was. I'd closed that box and put it on a shelf, and that box was so high that I couldn't reach it any more. But I pointed to it and said, *That is who I am.*

I am someone who hates exercise.

I am someone who hates feeling cold.

I am someone who doesn't like to be outside.

I am someone who doesn't like nature.

I am someone who is afraid of the sea.

I am someone who doesn't like change.

I left that box up on the shelf, year after year – even though I wanted to do something different, even though I wanted to get into the sea. I never thought it was an option to take the box down and see who I was now, at this moment. *Who am I today?* That voice in my head, like a mean girl, goaded me and teased me. If I even thought about doing something different or trying something new, the voice would come back. *That's not you, Georgie. Don't be a fool, don't embarrass yourself, don't even try because you will fail.* The voice pulled me back into my comfort zone, where I felt safe. And so, for years, I stayed the same.

And when we stay the same, life can feel out of flow. We become stagnant. Old stories, old truths, the past – it all starts to eat away at us. And it sits inside us, it lives there. Old pain. Old fear. And you go around and around. And around and around.

Even though I was sick and things were heavy, there was light. I could feel it. And what looked back at me in the mirror every day did not reflect how I felt on the inside. Because for the first time in as long as I could remember, I was no longer sleepwalking. I was *wide* awake. That's when I could see that this was my opportunity to rebuild my life with new stories. This felt like my chance to grab life with both hands.

But how do we really change?

When we are trying to start afresh, begin again, we are often trying to move away or change old ways. Things that no longer serve us.

The first step is to change your thoughts. When you change your thoughts, your actions follow. For example, if you tell yourself you are not fit, when will you get fit? If you tell yourself you are not a people person, how will you ever make new friends? If you tell yourself you are unhealthy, why would you make healthy choices?

Change the stories first, then the actions will follow.

So instead of saying:

I am unhealthy.

I make bad choices.

Change your language to:

I am healthy.

I make choices that nourish my body.

If you believe you are healthy, the next time it comes to making a decision, it will be easier to choose the healthy option.

After my cancer surgery I was determined to be the healthiest I could be, so I could give chemotherapy my best shot. I had a number of affirmations that I would repeat in the morning to reiterate what I knew was true. One of those was 'I make choices every day that nourish my body'. Every time I put something healthy into my body I visualised all the good it was doing internally. I knew the choices I was making were helping me and making me stronger.

And so, during chemotherapy, I was the healthiest I had ever been; although, when you looked at the external me, you would think I was very sick. I arrived at the hospital every Monday for my pre-chemo blood test, and every week I was told that my bloods were great. My haemoglobin levels were staying high, and each time

I got the go-ahead for another round of treatment. My nurses were so happy with how well I was doing. I really believed I was healthy. And the proof was in my blood.

And so, every decision I made between treatments was becoming easier. My main aim was to nourish my body when I could and when I had energy to do so. I had a smoothie with lots of greens in the morning alongside my breakfast, a healthy lunch and a hearty dinner. I didn't go on any diets. I didn't give up meat. I just added more fruit and vegetables to my diet and every day I drank two litres of water. My actions (making healthy decisions) mirrored my belief (I am healthy). Now that I've changed my beliefs to *I am healthy* and *I am hydrated*, I make decisions every day based on those beliefs. I smoked because I believed that was how I coped with stress. Smoking was my crutch. But when I got sick, my new reality was:

I am not a smoker.

Smoking has no place in my life.

I can cope with stress without smoking.

When I changed my thoughts around smoking, I stopped smoking. I could now see that I was surviving the most stressful situation of my life (my cancer diagnosis) without smoking.

After thirty-three years, my stories didn't have a hold

on me any more. All because I took them from my subconscious mind, acknowledged them and made a decision about whether they were still my truth or not.

My stories changed from:

I am not enough.

I am worthless.

I am undeserving.

I am unhealthy.

I can't …

I won't …

to:

I am enough.

I have enough.

I am worthy.

I am loved.

I am deserving.

I am healthy.

I am nourished.

I can …

I will …

When I believed I was healthy, I became healthier. When I felt worthy of living well and feeling well, I started to nourish my mind and body. When I changed my language, then changed my ways, I no longer felt less than.

We have to remember that if our thoughts stay the same, it is harder to change. We can't create a new life when we are held back by old stories. If you feel stuck and are sick of telling yourself the same stories, it could be time to take down your box, open it up and challenge everything that's inside. I got the job at 98FM because I changed my thoughts about myself. I finally loved myself, I was finally enough, I finally believed in myself. I knew I was worthy of great things. And because I took care of *my inner world first*, the rest followed. When you believe you are important and deserving, other people start to think you're important and deserving. That's when people start to take notice. That's when you get ahead. So going forward, make an effort to say nourishing things to yourself about yourself. Do it every day. And watch your world change.

In your journal, can you make a list of your 'I am's going forward?

> *I am loved.*
> *I am enough.*
> *I am strong.*
> *I am happy.*
> *I am feeling vulnerable and that's OK.*
> *I am unique.*
> *I am the hero of my own story.*

Affirmations

Each time you repeat an affirmation, imagine you are planting a seed in your mind. Promise you'll nourish and grow that seed.

- *I am on a journey of growth and change.*
- *I trust my inner wisdom.*
- *I am enough exactly as I am.*
- *I trust the process of life.*
- *I am confident.*
- *I am growing and changing for the better.*
- *I am worthy of all the good in my life.*
- *I am confident in my abilities.*
- *I am strong and powerful.*
- *I am calm and comfortable.*
- *I love the person I am becoming.*
- *I believe in myself.*
- *I am grateful for all that I have.*
- *I am courageous.*
- *I acknowledge all that I can achieve.*

Five steps to changing your story:

1 Know you are worthy of change

We often forget that we have the ability to change

enormously. We are made for change and it can bring great things to our lives. There will, of course, be ups and downs on a journey of growth. Days when you don't feel like 'doing' and that is perfectly OK. On those days, I let it all fall down and I don't judge myself. Deep down, I now have a belief that I am worthy of good things. I am worthy of being healthy and living a full and happy life. And knowing I am worthy keeps me curious, it reminds me to listen to my gut and gives me the courage to keep moving forward. To find new challenges, new experiences and to do things that scare me sometimes. No matter what age you are, know that change is possible. You have already come so far, you have already experienced challenges and one thing remains … you! Each morning when you open your eyes, believe that you can begin again. That you are not defined by your past. Change is possible and you can become all you are meant to be.

2 Let go to grow

I firmly believe that in order to step into the most powerful version of yourself, to make real, lasting changes, one of the first things you need to do is let go. Let go of the old ways, old beliefs and old stories that are holding you back. The person who you were yesterday, last month, ten years ago is not who you are today. Because replaying the past and holding on to old ways can stop us becoming who we are meant to be right now. So what do you need to let go of today? The belief that you are too old, too set in your ways, too weak? Do you believe you do not have enough time? That you are not good enough? That you are too afraid?

Often these beliefs are stopping you from experiencing life as you should. And like it or not, you are stopping your own growth! Once you let go of old beliefs and old stories you can make room for your new ones.

3 Cast your vote

Change can seem daunting and overwhelming sometimes. So get clear on how you can make change in a practical way. You can take steps forward by doing more things that align with the person you are looking to become.

Atomic Habits author James Clear says, 'Every action you take is a "vote" for the type of person you wish to become.'

It's interesting, isn't it? With each decision you make, you are simply showing up as the person you want to become.

For example, if you want to become

Healthier

More confident

Fitter

Hydrated

Ask yourself what votes you can cast for yourself today.

Healthier: make a nutritious soup.
More confident: pay a stranger a compliment.
Fitter: leave your runners by the front door.
Hydrated: drink a glass of water when you wake up.

Remember, big change comes from a collection of small decisions. So cast your votes, one at a time.

4   Stop waiting to start living

I love the story about the crabs in a bucket. It goes like this. Picture lots of crabs in a bucket. Eventually, one will try to escape. He'll climb up the side of the bucket, with one thing on his mind … freedom. But when the other crabs see him trying to escape, they don't like it. They'll try to bring him back, so they take hold of him, any part of him, and pull him down again. Because if they can't escape, they don't want anyone else to.

I often think we're afraid to do something different because it's easier to be a crab in a bucket. I was a crab in a bucket and I loved my bucket! Because there is comfort in doing the same things over and over again. There's friendship in the same – a culture, a tribe, a way.

But you are likely reading this book because you are on a journey of growth. You are curious and you are evolving.

If you feel in your heart that you want to do more, connect with that. Because it's time. It's time to get out of the bucket and do something different.

And here we are again, just changing course by one degree. Planting more seeds, stepping outside and seeing what else there could be for us. Choose one thing. What one thing can you do differently? Can you start casting votes for the person you want to become? Because that person is waiting for you. It's time to stop waiting and start living.

5 Explore new things

Now is your time to grow, to spread your wings. What have you always wanted to do? Where have you always wanted to go? Who have you always wanted to be? When you take yourself out of your box, you can see the infinite possibilities of the world. Write down what you would like to do and start casting votes to get there. Trust yourself, trust that there is more for you and trust your life. It is always creating miracles for you, but first you must believe.

A moment to pause

In the morning, take a few deep, intentional breaths.

You can do this standing or sitting.

When you feel settled, begin to visualise a mountain – maybe one you are familiar with or maybe the first image that comes into your mind.

Notice it's shape, the base of the mountain rooted into the earth, notice if it's steep or sloping.

And now, notice the weather patterns and changes on the mountain.

Night becomes day, day becomes night.

Seasons change, and the landscape changes with them.

Storms pass. People come and go.

And through all of the changes, the mountain sits, unmoved.

And know that we too can embody unwavering stillness in the face of change.

By becoming the mountain, we can link up with its strength and stability, adopting it for our own.

Always remembering that when difficult times arrive this too shall pass.

"

Life begins at the end
of your comfort zone.

"

Just One More Thing ...
Embrace The Cold

I was standing in my shower in 2020, feeling really low. My invisible string had come back, and I felt like it was pulling me down every morning. We were in lockdown, so the days were long and everything was just that bit harder. Harder to get up, harder to motivate myself to exercise, harder to find the positives in each day.

A few weeks before, Wim Hof had entered my life. You might have heard of him. He's one of the world's leading motivational speakers and inspires millions of people across the world to turn to the cold. And in his book, he speaks about how transformative the cold can be. So I decided to give cold showers a go to see if they would help me.

(Before you expose yourself to cold showers, it's always important to check with your medical professional – especially if you have an underlying condition. Do not try cold showers if you are pregnant.)

That day in 2020, after my lovely warm shower, I took a deep breath and, with shaky hands, turned the dial all the way down to cold. The whole family was there – Jamie, always so supportive, stood in the bathroom with a timer, Pia and the dog were there too. The cold took my breath away. I gasped for fifteen seconds and then turned off the water.

I can't describe the feeling as I stepped out of the shower. I was a new woman. I had been given a little shot of endorphins. In that moment, I felt part of something *bigger*. I looked in the mirror and stared at myself: *I can do hard things*. I was so proud. I had a spring in my step for the rest of the day.

Wim recommends doing a twenty-one-day challenge to build up the time. So I started to have cold showers every morning, and the fifteen seconds turned to two or three minutes after a couple of weeks.

After my cold shower, my day always looked brighter. I felt lighter. I could see the good in things much easier. I began to shake off that feeling of being pulled down, and slowly but surely my invisible string began to disappear.

The cold gave me a sense of accomplishment. It reminded me that I am capable of so much more than I think. When I feel low now, I know I need to change my energy, do something different. I need to break free from it. Sometimes we can get stuck, but I find when my energy changes, when I get my blood pumping or I do something that challenges me, I immediately feel better.

We all have this resource available to us, but it's much easier to stay in our comfort zones, where things are safe. However, when we step into the unknown, like into a cold shower or into nature, we unlock parts of ourselves that we never knew existed. That brave, strong person is in us all.

After that challenge, I could get into the sea with more confidence, and I used the cold showers to build me up, to prepare me. Soon enough, I would find myself craving the cold, because it became my reset button.

What's your reset button? Take some time to figure out what can help you reset yourself. Is it a cold shower, a walk on the beach, ten minutes outside without your phone? Get to know what you can do to help yourself feel better. Then you can use this in challenging times.

A couple of weeks later, Jamie had a big surprise for me. He had secretly got in touch with Wim's team and told them my story, and Wim had agreed to be a guest on *The Good Glow*! I couldn't believe it.

That day, the learnings came from Wim before he even started speaking. As we logged on to the call to begin our conversation, Wim was already there and I could hear him breathing. Big breath in, long breath out. In, out, in, out. Over and over again.

I felt nervous, like I had interrupted a sacred space – I didn't want to intrude. But he had already taught me my first lesson. *Give back to you before you give to others.* Centre yourself, make your world happy and calm, before you start giving.

We had a mind-blowing conversation about the benefits of cold water. He said a cold shower a day helps us connect with ourselves on a deeper level, that in a cold shower our cardiovascular system has the opportunity to connect with our deeper inner nature. Wim said, 'the investment in having a cold shower is small compared to the outcome' because you leave with 'a lot more energy and a lot less stress'.

I could feel this deep within – it had worked for me. Now, when that invisible string starts sneaking back into my life, I turn to the cold. The cold water is my biggest teacher. It is the biggest reminder of all I can be.

Stay Open

STEP ●●●● ❺

"

If it doesn't open,
it's not your door.

"

On 24 February 2022, I woke very early and reached for my phone like I had every morning that week. As quickly as my fingers would allow, I was on Twitter and refreshing my feed.

I blinked quickly as I read the news, not quite believing what I was seeing. My heart raced as I refreshed my feed over and over again. Hoping it was all a mistake.

Bombs.

Bombs were dropping on Kiev.

I jumped out of bed and ran to the living room. I turned on the news and watched in disbelief. I don't know if I moved from that spot for the next eighteen hours. My heart and my thoughts were with the people of Ukraine. I could only imagine how terrified they were feeling.

Our embryo transfer to our surrogate mother had been due to take place in Ukraine on Monday. This was Thursday. I tried to wake myself up, it felt like a nightmare, but it was real.

That week, everything blurred into one. I watched the news all day. I couldn't make dinner, I couldn't leave my house, I couldn't move. Takeaway boxes were stacking higher and higher. It's hard to admit, but I remember looking at Pia one evening and I just couldn't remember if I had fed her. My brain wasn't working. It felt like the world had stopped spinning.

In 2020, Jamie and I started speaking about expanding our family and the various options we had. It had been over two years since my diagnosis, and we were eager for Pia to have a sibling. We decided that instead of coming off my cancer drug, Tamoxifen, to have a baby naturally, we would use our frozen embryos to pursue surrogacy.

A few months beforehand, I was sitting in a hair salon and, over my shoulder, I saw Rosanna Davison. Rosanna had recently announced that she and her husband Wesley were expecting a baby via surrogate. That day, she shared with me that her journey was taking place in Ukraine. I looked at her in complete awe. She was willing to share her journey with the world. I wondered if she had any idea of the incredible impact she was having. Rosanna was paving the way for me and other women to walk the same path. Over the next couple of weeks we started the process, and I naively thought I would have a baby (or twins!) in my arms within the year.

Everything took much longer than expected but thankfully a year later, in August 2021, six of our precious embryos left the Beacon Hospital in Dublin and were brought by special courier to Ukraine.

Just thinking of my little embryos sitting at the traffic lights in Sandyford blew my mind. I felt extremely emotional that week. I'd liked knowing they were close to us but now they were across the world. However, I knew that once our embryos arrived safely in Kiev, our clinic would be able to start the process of matching us with a surrogate mother.

We were getting closer and closer to holding our precious baby in our arms. But time was ticking by and we heard nothing. Each week, I hoped there would be some good news. It felt like everything was taking such a long time. The more time passed, the more my heart ached for a baby.

That December, my mother-in-law, Hazel, rented a chalet in France and treated us to a week in the snowy mountains. I had never spent Christmas away from home, but we were so excited to go on this trip of a lifetime with Jamie's family. I am as obsessed with his family as with my own. Jamie's sister Julie had become a sister to me from the minute I'd met her, and I love them all, Jamie's brother Jason and his wife Jean, Julie's husband JP and my niece and nephews. We set off on 19 December, and it was chaos from the moment we met at the airport, but in the best possible way. It was magic. It was Hazel's dream to have all of her grandchildren together for Christmas, so this was a really special trip.

As we sat on the plane waiting to take off, I felt a pang in my heart. Christmas was upon us and we still hadn't matched with a surrogate. The thought of starting another year no closer to our second baby was overwhelming at times. But as always, I was finding a way to trust the process.

As the plane rumbled down the runway I opened a book by Louise Hay called *Trust Life*. It had been on my shelf for quite some time, and something told me to pack it in my hand luggage. As we took off and flew above the clouds, I held the book close to my chest and thought, *whatever page it lands on is the one I am supposed to read today.*

I flicked through it and picked a page. When I looked down I could see the title of the page was 'I Have All the Time in the World'.

Louise said: 'Time is exactly what I make it to be … When we can see the perfection of each experience, then we are never rushed or delayed. We are in the right place at the right time, and all is well.'

Wow. In that moment, I heard it loud and clear. I closed the book, I let go of expectations, I let go of the worry and stress that I was running out of time. I decided to focus on what I had in front of me, my gorgeous little Pia, and the wonderful experience we were about to have as a family.

I allowed myself to surrender to whatever was next and trust that everything that was meant for me was on its way.

I have come to believe that when you finally let something go, when you finally decide not to hold on so tightly, an incredible life will reveal itself to you.

A few days later, we had stopped for lunch at our favourite place on the side of the Alps. It was burgers all round and the kids were so excited. Tomorrow was Christmas Eve.

I checked my emails, and there was one from our agency. Just sitting there in my inbox. I opened it and there was the news we had been waiting for all year. We had been matched with a surrogate. I opened the attachment on the email and there was a picture of the woman I had been waiting for. An earth angel.

Her name was Alina. I read all about her life and I stared at her picture. She was the one. I knew straight away.

I ran to Jamie, who was taking pictures of the kids, and I grabbed his arm. I explained what had happened and I said, 'This is her, Jamie. She is the one.' I told him

I was writing back straight away to say YES, a million times over.

I knew we had found her and she had found us.

The following morning, Christmas Eve, we confirmed everything. It was official: we had found someone who was willing to carry our baby. The next few days, as you can imagine, were absolutely perfect. It felt like a real-life Christmas miracle.

When we got home from France a couple of days later, I printed off Alina's picture, folded it into a small box, and put that box into a bigger box, and a bigger box, and so on.

I hadn't told my family that we had been matched because I needed to see their reactions. I needed to be with them when they heard the news.

We were off to my mum's house for dinner, and I wanted to surprise my family with the news. As my stepdad Joe opened each box and finally straightened out the piece of paper, he turned it around and showed it to my mum, my two brothers Mick and Sam, and their partners Ciara and Sophie. They turned to me with their mouths open.

'Who is that?' they asked.

'It's our surrogate mother!' I answered.

The sound of their screams is something I'll never

forget. The celebrations, the love, the joy. It was the most magical moment – all of our dreams came true during Christmas 2021. We were about to go on the most amazing adventure.

When I look back to that time, none of it felt quite real. I protected myself a lot by not getting too excited. I had to take it one step at a time, so I continued planning my year as normal. It was almost like I was removed from it all. Alina was given a plan by the doctor and we were due to transfer our embryo to her on 21 February. As we moved into February, those close to me started to delicately bring up the elephant in the room. The one I was choosing to ignore, the situation between Russia and Ukraine. I kept telling people that we had faith things would be okay. The word from Ukraine was that there would be no invasion and things were to continue as normal.

But as the days passed, and it started to make headline news, it was time to acknowledge what was almost too painful to think about. I was watching the news every day and US President Joe Biden was insisting that Vladimir Putin would invade Kiev. Things were getting more and more serious. The people of Ukraine were in very real danger.

On Thursday, 17 February, Senator Mary Seery Kearney hosted an emergency meeting with parents pursuing surrogacy in Ukraine. I was speaking at an event on Zoom that night, so I reminded Jamie to log on to the meeting so we could stay up-to-date with the situation. At 10 p.m. I closed my laptop after a lovely couple of hours, and I made my way down the hall to find Jamie.

When I turned the corner into our bedroom, I stopped dead in my tracks. His face spoke a thousand words. When I looked at him, I knew it was bad, bad news. Jamie doesn't normally get rattled but I could see that he was freaking out. He turned to me and said, 'We can't go ahead, Georgie, it's really serious. He started speaking about a war, and what if we couldn't find Alina or the baby. It was so hard to process it all in that moment. This was so much more serious than I thought.

He said it had been relayed on the call that there was a strong indication that Russia was going to invade Ukraine, and if possible, we should pause our journey.

I looked at him like he was out of his mind. This could not be happening. I couldn't believe the words that were coming out of his mouth. We were due to transfer in four days!

'There has to be a way, Jamie?'

'No,' he said.

And I knew by the tone of his voice that I would never

in a million years change his mind. That night he said there was absolutely no way the embryo transfer could go ahead on Monday.

We sent an email to our clinic that night asking them to pause our journey and asked if they could speak to us first thing the next morning.

When I went to bed that night, I felt like Jamie had broken my heart. It wasn't his fault of course, but it was just so hard to let all the hope we'd had go.

The following morning, I had to force myself to leave the house. I had an acupuncture appointment, a treatment I had started to help with anxiety, at 9.30 a.m. and I needed to go to the shops beforehand, as we were hosting Pia's fifth birthday party that weekend. I wanted to be at home with Jamie but mine was the first appointment of the day at the acupuncture clinic so I had no way to cancel – and I didn't want to just not show up. I walked around Dunnes in a daze. It was quite early in the morning and I was standing in the cereal aisle staring at the Rice Krispies when my phone rang. It was Jamie. He sounded panicked.

In the last few minutes, he had taken a call from our agency in Ukraine. They told him that Alina wanted to continue the journey. She had taken the medication and her body was ready for a transfer. They agency said she would be assigned to another family who wanted to proceed, if we didn't go ahead on Monday.

Considering the amount of time I spend in my house, I couldn't believe I was getting this news in aisle ten of the supermarket. I quickly hung up, paid for my shopping and ran to the car. I called Jamie back and said we had to find a way to keep Alina, because she was the one. I felt a complete desperation running through my body. I've never felt anything like it. If Alina was in front of me, I would have got down on my hands and knees and begged her to wait for us. I was driving towards Blackrock, and all I wanted to do was scream. I didn't know what to do or who to trust. Our agency was telling us that Russia wouldn't invade, that we were being too cautious. So it was really hard to know if we were making the right decision.

So I arrived at the clinic in a complete panic. I walked into the room, lay down on the bed and Janette, my therapist, looked down at me. It was the last place I wanted to be on Earth. She noticed the look on my face and asked if I was OK. I looked up at her, my eyes filled with tears, and I just couldn't speak. Frozen, a feeling I was all too familiar with.

No words left my mouth, but in that moment she

took my hand in hers, held it close to her chest and said, 'Don't worry, Georgie, people come here with broken hearts all the time.'

How did she know?

She got to work, placed the needles in all the right places, and left the room for half an hour. I didn't want her to go, I didn't want to be left alone.

The first few minutes were torture. I felt like ripping everything out of my body and running out the door. Down the street. As far away as possible. I felt so overwhelmed and so out of control. I was being forced to lie there in complete silence, no distractions, no phone, just me, for thirty agonising minutes.

Now I can see that it was the greatest gift I could have been given at that moment. Now I can see that I was meant to be there.

My mind was a muddled, panicked mess. I couldn't think straight. But as I lay there, all of a sudden something came over me. Peace. And as the minutes ticked by there was a feeling of guidance, a feeling of knowing. Overwhelming clarity. I had stopped, I had embraced the silence, and now I knew what I had to do.

That day, a version of me walked into the clinic and a different one emerged an hour later.

I don't know quite what happened there, but a sense of calm came over me. In just an hour of silence, I felt entirely different about the situation and I knew what I needed to do.

As I walked towards my car, I picked up my phone and called Jamie. I said, 'We have to let Alina go, Jamie, we have to let her go.'

By stopping and embracing the silence, by connecting with myself, I could see it all so clearly. I could see that I was making the best choice for my family, and Alina was making the best choice for hers.

I love the expression 'we are all just walking each other home'. Gerry says it from time to time. And I could see it that day, we are walking each other home. We are all on our own individual journeys. And it's not for me to say what Alina should do on hers.

And how different the world could be if we could just see that. If we made each other's journeys a little easier. If we came to each other from a place of understanding and love.

Wouldn't the world be a better place if we could just remember to do that?

So I let it all fall down.

I let go.

I could see that none of this was in my control.

I won't say the next couple of weeks were easy. Especially when the worst happened. The unimaginable. I watched the news around the clock. I prayed for Alina and her family. I prayed for all the people we had been working with who were now living in bunkers. I prayed for the embryologist who had rescued our embryos. I prayed for every single person in Ukraine who was suffering.

I watched along with the rest of the world in horror. At times, it was hard to believe that we could stand by and watch such pain, such devastation. It felt inhuman. My whole heart was there.

When it was time to think about our second baby and what could have been, I had to find a way to let go of that journey, that embryo, everything that I thought was waiting for us. The grief was enormous. I couldn't stop thinking about who that little person would have become.

The pain lasted longer than I expected, but I sat in it and I asked for help. And through that time, as the months passed, I found a way to let go.

And I knew in time that I would be able to see a new path. Even though I couldn't see it right away, I trusted it would emerge. Sometimes, I think the only way we can get through the tough times is to trust in something more.

We hoped and prayed for peace, for those being devastated by war in Ukraine. Jamie and my family tried to help me see that maybe our journey with Ukraine was over. Even typing these words is heartbreaking. Ukraine will always have a piece of my heart.

But when I think back to the day of my acupuncture appointment, and how I allowed myself to let go, I can see how different I am now. Before 2017, when things didn't go my way, it ate away at me. I fell hard, I took it personally, I told myself I had no luck or that bad things 'always' happened to me. I tried to find a way to blame myself, like there was something wrong with me. I couldn't learn from the hard times, because I always wanted to push them away. Underneath it all, I didn't believe I had the ability to rebuild. I didn't trust myself enough. I didn't trust my journey.

So in time, when I came to a place of acceptance after the grief, I was able to pick myself up. And I allowed myself to see where I could go next.

✳

So how can we surrender? Remember, when you surrender, you are not giving up. Surrendering is about releasing the outcome and making space for the life you are supposed to live. When you surrender you make space for miracles to happen and you are no longer resisting what is meant for you.

One day, I was speaking at a corporate event and somebody asked, 'Why did I not get the promotion last week and what do I do now?'

I replied, 'So why didn't you get the new role? The answer is that this job is not meant for you right now. So it's time to figure out *what else* you can do. What else is calling for you? Can you put the energy you were going to put into the new role back into yourself? Because maybe that's what you need now.

'What is *your* opportunity from this situation? The universe is trying to tell you something, and it's up to you to listen, if you are willing.'

What happens when you work against the flow of your life?

I spent twelve years waiting for a job in 98FM. I worked extra hours; I never took a break, I gave it all up for one outcome that I became fixated on.

And then the stories came: *I'll be happy once I get the job. I'll be healthier once I get the job. Life will start once I get the job.*

I interviewed for it, but never got it. I decided to wait, resisting the idea that there was another possible path for me.

But what if we allowed ourselves to surrender after rejection?

What if we could see that rejection is sometimes protection?

That maybe the universe wants to bring us somewhere else?

What if, instead of waiting, we focused on our own growth?

What if we opened up our world?

Found a way to trust life?

Now I can see I was never supposed to get the job.

So next time you get a no, can you ask yourself WHY?

Five steps to living in flow:

① Acknowledge

The power to acknowledge your life how it is, is one of the greatest tools for growth. We often keep ourselves so busy and distracted by the day to day, that we don't make time to look at the bigger picture of our lives. We have no time to ask ourselves the important questions like: Who am I? Where am I going? What am I actually trying to achieve?

If we give ourselves *time and space* to look at our lives, when we are in a place of feeling centred and calm, we will avoid making decisions out of fear or panic.

Can you make the time to be open to listening to what your life is trying to tell you? Life can often speak to us through whispers – that little voice in the back of your mind. Often, these whispers get louder and louder until they whack us right over the head. Remember in the lead-up to my diagnosis, I couldn't put my finger on what was wrong with me when I was looking in the mirror? I can see now that I was getting the whisper to get checked out, but I ignored it.

We often push certain thoughts away because they can feel too scary or too big. But it's important if you want to change or take yourself forward in life that you get real about where you are. Are you really happy? Are you trying to force something that maybe isn't meant for you? Is it time for a change? What have you been ignoring for too long?

This is such a brave and empowering thing to do and will only help you in the long term. Acknowledgement is liberating.

2 Accept it

In order to *change* your life, you must first *be accepting of your life.*

One of the greatest things you can do for yourself is free yourself from thinking that things need to be or should be a certain way.

Can you stop labelling things as the right way or wrong way and just be? If we look at everything as either 'good' or 'bad' or 'right' or 'wrong', we can get stuck, unsure of where to go or what to do. That can sometimes lead to being too afraid to make any decisions at all.

When we detach and let go of how things *should be,*

then we can make way for curiosity and exploration. We'll enjoy the journey of life more. Let's face it, life rarely works out the way we intend. But when we let go, that's when truly amazing things can happen.

I know from my life, when I'm in the depths of it, I can't see an experience for what it truly is until much later. It's only later that we gain perspective.

If we can find a way to be open and accepting of where life could be taking us, the destination could be more than you could have ever dreamed of.

Silence can help us with acceptance. Sit with yourself, let thoughts pass through you, make peace with yourself and allow space for miracles to happen.

As Eckhart Tolle says in his book *Stillness Speaks*, 'It is inner stillness that will save and transform the world.'

3 Swap caution for courage

Can you find a way with being OK for things to be different to what you are used to? Comfort zones keep us safe, but what if we were willing to step out of our comfort zones? What if we were open to stepping into the unknown? This can be uncomfortable, but it's supposed to be. This is where the growth is. This is when you will start evolving.

Some of us stay in relationships, friendships and jobs that are not making us happy deep down. We are willing to sacrifice our own growth, our own journeys, just because it's easier when things stay the same. We often avoid changing things up because we fear the disruption it could bring to our lives. But what if short-term disruption leads to long-term happiness? A new way, a new world, a new life?

Something important to remember: do all you can, then let it go. When you stop forcing your life to go in a certain direction, you allow space to bring in more. Maybe something else is waiting for you. Trust the process and be open to a new way.

If you find it difficult to trust, this is a great opportunity to seek guidance by asking for a sign. Signs are not for everybody and that's OK, but if you feel called to ask for one, then do. When we get our sign it can often empower and encourage us to trust that all is happening as it should. And if we don't get our sign, that can be a sign in itself too.

4 Hand it over

When you hang on too tight, or you are forcing something to go in a certain direction, do you ever feel like you are suffering? There is enormous freedom in releasing yourself from the pressure of trying to make things work the way you think they should. It can be so liberating to give yourself a break and hand it over. You don't have to suffer in this space. Free up your energy for something else. Something that will bring more to your life, instead of taking from it.

5 Feel the freedom

Letting go is a huge step; acknowledge this and love yourself. Always know that you can come back to your affirmations to centre yourself and remind yourself to trust the process.

Affirmations I turn to when I need guidance

- *The universe has a plan greater than mine.*
- *I am willing to see where my life is taking me.*
- *I gently release my need for control.*
- *I choose not to live in fear.*
- *I welcome change with open arms.*
- *I accept myself, I love myself, and I'm moving forward.*

A moment to pause

When you feel challenged or overwhelmed that something isn't working out as you had wanted it to or had planned, take a deep breath and check in with yourself.

Ask yourself what is here for me right now? In body, in breath, resting and being here in this moment?

You don't have to figure anything out or do anything, just for these moments of stillness.

Can you soften and just be?

Can we find surrender in these moments?

When we surrender to a trust that things are happening for us, the universe often delivers outcomes greater than we could have ever imagined.

Can you allow this greater plan to unfold for you?

Can you trust that everything you hope for is on its way to you if you open yourself to how it unfolds?

Try to connect with this feeling of trust and remind yourself that the universe is guiding you and will bring you to a place far greater than you ever could have imagined.

“

Surrender every day.

”

Evening Ritual

We live in a world where we're led to believe that surrendering is a sign of weakness. And when we think about surrendering, we often think of failure. But I surrender every day and it feels so good. I no longer see surrendering as a weakness: I see it as a strength. So what if we embraced it?

What if we set a cut-off time in our day? We are not built to be 'on' all the time, so to have the awareness to know when you have given enough is huge. This is something we need to encourage and tap into within ourselves.

Dr Libby Weaver is one of the world's leading female-health experts. She has given a TED talk and written bestselling books. She is particularly interested in stress and the impact it can have on our bodies. She describes our sympathetic nervous system, which drives 'fight or flight' mode, as the red zone, and the parasympathetic nervous system, which is often referred to as rest, digest and repair mode, as the green zone.

As our worlds become busier and more stressful, we find ourselves spending more time in the red zone, and some of us even get stuck there. So somebody who is chronically stressed will spend more time in the red zone.

At certain times, it is important for us to be in the red zone – for example, when we feel a threat or unsafe. It's our stress response and can help us out in tricky situations.

But as important as the red zone is *at times*, we need to allow our bodies to move into the green zone. In the green zone, our bodies slow down and we enter a state of relaxation. This is when our body can function as it's supposed to and we can recover. When the parasympathetic nervous system is activated, we are calm.

I believe I lived in the red zone for more than ten years. I was constantly stressed, with my adrenaline pumping, and I had an elevated heart rate throughout the day. I was always frantic and never gave my body a chance to recover or reset.

Now that I am aware of the green zone, and the benefits of it, I try to get into that zone as often as I can. The quickest way to move from the red zone to the green zone is by extending the length of our exhalation. Try it now and notice how you feel afterwards.

- Inhale through your nostrils and feel your belly expanding outwards.
- Pause at the end of the inhalation.
- Now slowly exhale through your nostrils and feel your tummy shrinking back towards your spine.

By doing this, you have communicated to every cell in your body that you're safe.

You can come back to this exercise anytime you feel stressed, anytime you feel overwhelmed. It is a tool I use in the evening to move out of my working day.

What's your quitting time?

Set a time of the day to stop. By setting a quitting time, you are letting yourself and the people around you know that you have done enough today.

My quitting time is 8 p.m, about two hours before I go to bed. At 8 p.m., I down tools. I surrender. I relax. I switch off. I breathe. At 8 p.m., I am ready for the green zone. By creating a quitting time, you are setting boundaries.

Boundaries are something that I didn't have before. I believe this was one of the reasons why I lived in the red zone for so long. Remember, just because you *can* keep giving doesn't mean you *should*.

By setting a quitting time, you are setting a boundary for yourself. And boundaries help us define our limits, they help preserve and protect our energy. Boundaries can help us align with ourselves and identify how much we can give and how much we cannot. Setting them doesn't make you selfish: it makes you stronger. We need to remember that our energy is precious, and we need to protect it.

Boundaries help other people understand how to behave with you. They draw a line in the sand that you don't let other people cross. At the same time, as important as *setting* boundaries is, it is also important to *communicate* what your boundaries are. That way, people know your limitations.

A few things to consider are:

- Do you take calls from a friend late at night? Does this friend spend the phone call speaking about their life, never asking you about yours? Be careful of what energy you let into your space, especially before bed.
- Does your child hand you their dirty sports clothes just before bed and expect them to be washed and ready for the following day? Are you staying up late

to finish jobs that could have been done earlier?

- Does your boss send you emails late at night? Does this put you back into work mode? Could one of your boundaries be to *not* check your emails past a certain time?

My friends and family wouldn't dream of calling me at night, because they know I switch off and enjoy going to bed early. In the same way, I wouldn't send someone I work with an email outside of work hours. And even though Jamie is the opposite to me, and his creative brain is awakened at night, he knows not to talk to me about work past 8 p.m.

By setting a quitting time for myself, I often have a more productive evening. Because knowing there's a cut-off point helps me use my time more efficiently. Having a small amount of time to clear up after dinner and get ready for the next day helps me stay on track. If I didn't have a quitting time, I know my to-do list would continue late into the night.

It can be hard to stick to quitting time, because we are often willing to sacrifice our personal time for the 'greater good' of the household. But something I have come to realise is that, no matter how hard I try, my house will never be tidy. There, I said it! So I have given up putting so much of my personal time into trying to keep it that way. I surrender to the mess sometimes, because my health is more important. And so is yours.

Once I down tools, I can catch up on my skincare, have a bath, read my book or watch something on TV. I never watch the news at night – I like to protect this sacred time, do nice things and invite the calm in. I love to go to bed early with a herbal tea and listen to a short meditation before I fall asleep. I have come a long way from needing to watch something on TV to get to sleep. Weekends, of course, are different. I'll have a glass of wine with Jamie or catch up with friends. But my weekday evenings are slow. A chance to rest, a chance to focus on my healthy habits, and a chance to fill my cup.

Things to think about

- Do you spend more time in the red zone or the green zone?
- Could you create a breathing or meditation practice to help you transition into the green zone?
- What time could your quitting time be?
- What boundaries could you put in place for yourself in the evening?

"

I have the power
to be the hero
of my own story.

"

Just One More Thing ...
Be Unapologetically You

'Many times when you try to change, there is a whole circle of people who actually like you better the old way.' This quote from Oprah's book *The Path Made Clear* really speaks to me, because when we are in the process of change it can be hard. Hard for us and hard for those around us.

When you spend years labelling yourself, people expect you to show up in a certain way. So when you start something new, it can be uncomfortable for people.

Say, for example, you take up meditation. People around you could easily say, 'You've changed! This is *so* bizarre – you're not the type of person to meditate!' Or they could go a little further. They might make a joke about it. Then we might feel shame or embarrassment. This can be why some of us keep ourselves small. Because changing makes you feel vulnerable. And for other people, your change could be highlighting what's not changing in them.

When we are in transition we could have thoughts like:

- What will people think of me?
- I have been the same way for so long, what if I change and then I am rejected?

When I was in the process of change I called it out. I said to Jamie, 'I am going to start running and I need you to support and encourage me – this is a big deal for me.' And he did. He encouraged and loved me. He supported my change, as did my family and Jamie's family. I felt so lucky.

But I did lose some friends in my wider circle during my transition. People always say you know who your friends are when the chips are down. But I think it's the opposite. And I'm going to tell you why. People will always come by when you are drowning. Some people will happily sit with you in the pain. All day.

But what happens when you flip it? What about when things start to go well? What about when you start to get your wings? When you start to soar? When you rise?

Are they still there?

So I think you know who your friends are when the chips are up.

It can be hard to deal with this. When things are going

well or you are on a journey of growth, you want people to be happy for you. But that's not always the way. And what you do next is what is really important. So don't hold yourself back because you are afraid of how others will react if you soar. Don't keep yourself small so other people can feel comfortable. Don't dim your light because people are not used to it shining so bright.

I now look at life like it's a series of chapters. Some people stay in the same chapter. They read the same pages over and over again. And that is OK. But that doesn't have to be your story. Because we get one shot, and guess what? You have the power to keep turning the pages.

Be unapologetically you and follow your heart.

Remember, this is your light and your life, so let it shine bright.

The Best Is Yet To Come – Conclusion

I created this book in the hope of helping you see that your precious life is waiting to be lived – that your dream life can be anything you wish it to be. The steps in this book, just like our journeys, are ever-evolving. We are born to grow, to learn and to create.

Every dawn brings the opportunity to begin again, to see the world for the first time, to rediscover who you are. I want to remind you that you already have everything you need to create your dream life.

We can spend a lifetime looking outside of ourselves, always searching for more. We can live like this until we take our last breath. Or we can stop and choose to see it a different way.

When I was told I was sick, I wasn't thinking about my job title, how much money was in my bank account or what bag I carried on my arm. I wasn't thinking about what other people thought of me, or who they wanted me to be. I thought about the people I love. Nothing mattered more than the moments I had lived with them, and the moments I had yet to live.

I thought of my daughter's eyes, her beating heart, every smile, every embrace, every precious moment together.

And then I realised that all I had been searching for, I had already found.

The pursuit of 'more' can be fickle. Because more is never enough. More is infinite, it's never-ending. And so you have a choice: you can keep searching, or you can choose to see that you are enough.

We can get caught in a cycle. Searching outside of ourselves for acceptance, searching for more love, more respect, more appreciation. You can search and search down an endless path. But once you stop and find acceptance and love and respect and appreciation within yourself, all of a sudden your world starts overflowing with those exact things.

Then it becomes clear. The world is simply holding up a mirror to who we are and who we choose to be. So that acceptance – the love, the respect and the appreciation – starts showing up in abundance. It's everywhere we turn.

Can you trust your life enough to step forward? Trust that life will show you just how beautiful it can be?

Choose to see that every moment is precious? Choose to see that there can be no darkness without light?

Can you remember that every morning the sun rises again? And that the small things in life could actually be the big things?

Can you remind yourself to be happy when the happiness is taking place? And know that these very moments are soon ones you will call the good old days?

And when the rock bottom moments come, and they will come, can you see them not as the end, but as an opportunity to begin again?

Can you remember that hope and love and trust and belief all come from within? And with that hope, with that love, with that trust and belief, you can start to create the life of your dreams?

And, yes, your dreams will need work. Your dreams will need commitment and a willingness to learn. Your dreams will challenge you. Your dreams will require you to ask for help, to get uncomfortable, to dig deep. They will dare you to finally step into the unknown.

But what is waiting for you on the other side is a life greater than you could have ever imagined.

We are born with so much belief, but the opposite is learned along the way. So it's now time for less doubts, less fear, less waiting.

Because you matter. Your dreams and your ambitions, they matter. But first you need to believe that you are worthy. Because no one will believe in you, until you first believe in yourself.

So what's it going to be?

The choice is yours.

Your life is waiting for you.

Is it time to go live it?

Bibliography

Atomic Habits: Tiny Changes, Remarkable Results by James Clear (Random House Business, 2018)

Resisting Happiness by Matthew Kelly (Beacon Publishing, 2016)

Stillness Speaks by Eckhart Tolle (New World Library, 2003)

The Body Keeps The Score by Bessel van der Kolk (Penguin Books, 2015)

The Path Made Clear by Oprah Winfrey (Blue Bird, 2019)

The Power of I AM: Two Words That Will Change Your Life Today by Joel Osteen (FaithWords, 2016)

The Universe Has Your Back by Gabrielle Bernstein (Hay House UK, 2016)

Tony Robbins: I Am Not Your Guru. Directed by Joe Berlinger (Netflix, 2016)

Trust Life: Love Yourself Every Day with Wisdom from Louise Hay by Louise Hay (Hay House UK, 2018)

What I Know for Sure by Oprah Winfrey (Macmillan, 2014)

Acknowledgements

Where do I begin? As someone who has loved writing since I was a little girl, this has been one of the greatest experiences of my life.

But one I couldn't have done without my family.

To my daughter Pia, you are my everything. I hope this book reminds you that you are capable of anything. Shine bright, little girl. I will always be with you.

To Jamie, my husband, my best friend, my life coach (I could go on and on). Nothing is possible without you. Thank you for all the five-star moments. I am always excited for our next chapter.

To my mum and Joe, the world is a greater place with you in it. I am so proud to be your daughter. Words can never describe my love for you.

Mick, Sam, Ciara and Sophie, I am so grateful for the love you give me. I adore you all.

Hazel, Julie, JP, Jason and Jean, my name may not begin with a J, but you make me feel like it does. The best in-laws I could ever ask for.

Alanna, James, Joshua, Jacob, Finn and Olive. My nieces and nephews, watching the world through your eyes is magic. Thank you for everything you have taught me. I will always be here for you all.

My dad and Julie, thank you for the love and support.

My agent, Dave, thank you for everything you do for me. You are like family. I am so grateful.

My editor Ciara, Joanna, Elaine, and all the team at Hachette, thank you for believing in this book and seeing my vision for it.

Thank you to Emma, Aonghus and Karen for your work on the book. And to Nic&Lou for the beautiful cover.

To The Good Glow community, you have given me such purpose over the last five years. The friendship, the tears, the support, the love, the laughs, you make my life better. I adore the moments we meet.

To Professor Hill, thank you for saving my life. I get to live it because of you.

I have recorded some
guided meditations which
connect to the five steps I explore
in this book. These meditations
can be found at

www.thegoodglow.ie/glow